The Enchilada Kitchen

Discover the Best Enchilada Recipes for Authentic, Spicy, and Mouthwatering Mexican Cuisine.

Jonathan Richardson

Copyright Material ©2023

All Rights Reserved

Without the proper written consent of the publisher and copyright owner, this book cannot be used or distributed in any way, shape, or form, except for brief quotations used in a review. This book should not be considered a substitute for medical, legal, or other professional advice.

TABLE OF CONTENTS

TABLE OF CONTENTS 3
INTRODUCTION 6
CHEESE ENCHILADAS 7
1. Basic Cheese Enchiladas 8
2. Creamy Cheese Enchiladas 10
3. Spinach and Cheese Enchiladas 12
4. Three-Cheese Enchiladas 14
5. Black Bean and Cheese Enchiladas 16
6. Roasted Vegetable and Cheese Enchiladas 18
7. White Cheese Enchiladas 20
8. Beef and Cheese Enchiladas 22
9. Spinach and Cheese Enchiladas 24
10. Shrimp and Cheese Enchiladas 26
11. Chicken and Cheese Enchiladas with Verde Sauce 28
12. Vegetarian Black Bean and Cheese Enchiladas 30
BEEF ENCHILADAS 32
13. Basic Beef Enchiladas 33
14. Beef and Bean Enchiladas 35
15. Spicy Beef Enchiladas 37
16. Beef Enchiladas with Homemade Sauce 39
17. Beef Enchiladas with Green Sauce 41
18. Slow Cooker Beef Enchiladas 43
19. Beef Enchiladas with Creamy Sauce 45
20. Beef Enchiladas with Mole Sauce 47
21. Beef Enchiladas with Chipotle Sauce 49
22. Beef Enchiladas with Tomatillo Sauce 51
23. Beef Enchiladas with Ranchero Sauce 53
24. Beef Enchiladas with Green Chile Sauce 55
25. Beef Enchiladas with Salsa Verde 57
26. Beef Enchiladas with Pico de Gallo 59
27. Beef Enchiladas with Mole Sauce 61
28. Beef Enchiladas with Chipotle Sauce 63
CHICKEN ENCHILADAS 65
29. Basic Chicken Enchiladas 66
30. Chicken and Spinach Enchiladas 68
31. Green Chile Chicken Enchiladas 70

32. Creamy Chicken Enchiladas 72
33. Red Chile Chicken Enchiladas 74
34. Spicy Chicken Enchiladas 76
35. Cheesy Chicken Enchiladas 78
36. Creamy Chicken Enchiladas with Poblano Sauce 80
37. Chicken Enchiladas with Verde Sauce 83
38. Creamy Chicken Enchiladas with Tomatillo Sauce 85

FISH AND SEAFOOD 88
39. Shrimp Enchiladas 89
40. Crab Enchiladas 91
41. Seafood Enchiladas 93
42. Salmon Enchiladas 95
43. Grilled Fish Enchiladas 97
44. Tuna Enchiladas 99
45. Mahi-Mahi Enchiladas 101

VEGETABLE ENCHILADAS 104
46. Vegetarian Enchiladas 105
47. Spinach and Mushroom Enchiladas 107
48. Sweet Potato and Black Bean Enchiladas 109
49. Roasted Vegetable Enchiladas 111
50. Cauliflower Enchiladas 113
51. Black Bean and Corn Enchiladas 115
52. Butternut Squash and Spinach Enchiladas 117
53. Zucchini and Corn Enchiladas 119
54. Portobello Mushroom Enchiladas 121

VEGAN ENCHILADAS 123
55. Vegan Black Bean and Corn Enchiladas 124
56. Vegan Chickpea Enchiladas 126
57. Vegan Sweet Potato Enchiladas 128
58. Vegan Spinach and Tofu Enchiladas 130
59. Vegan Jackfruit Enchiladas 132
60. Vegan Lentil Enchiladas 134
61. Vegan Tempeh Enchiladas 136
62. Vegan Sweet Potato Enchiladas 138
63. Vegan Quinoa Enchiladas 140

FRUIT ENCHILADAS 142
64. Strawberry Cream Cheese Enchiladas 143
65. Pineapple Enchiladas 145

66. Apple Enchiladas 147
67. Mixed Berry Enchiladas 149
68. Peach Enchiladas 151

LEGUMES AND GRAINS 153
69. Quinoa Enchilada Casserole 154
70. Sweet Potato and Black Bean Enchiladas 156
71. Black Bean Enchiladas 158
72. Mixed Bean Enchiladas 160

SAUCES 162
73. Easy Red Enchilada Sauce 163
74. Red Enchilada Sauce 165
75. Green Enchilada Sauce 167
76. Ancho Chili Enchilada Sauce 169
77. Roasted Tomato Enchilada Sauce 171
78. Chipotle Enchilada Sauce 173
79. Creamy Enchilada Sauce 175
80. Smoky Enchilada Sauce 177
81. Mole Enchilada Sauce 179
82. Ranchero Enchilada Sauce 181
83. White Enchilada Sauce 183
84. Whiskey Chipotle Enchilada Sauce 185
85. Vegan Cashew Cheese Sauce 187
86. Fresh Tomato Salsa 1
87. Spicy Mango And Red Pepper Salsa 2
88. Chipotle-Tomato Salsa 1
89. Pineapple-Papaya Salsa 2
90. Tomatillo Salsa 2
91. Salsa Verde 1
92. Roasted Red Salsa 1
93. Tomatillo Enchilada Sauce 3
94. Pasilla Enchilada Sauce 5
95. Three Pepper Enchilada Sauce 7
96. Ancho Enchilada Sauce 9
97. Guajillo Enchilada Sauce 11
98. Mole Enchilada Sauce 13
99. Salsa Verde Enchilada Sauce 15
100. Green Chile Enchilada Sauce 17

CONCLUSION 19

INTRODUCTION

Welcome to The Enchilada Kitchen, where we celebrate the vibrant and diverse flavors of Mexico through the delicious and comforting dish of enchiladas. In this cookbook, you'll find 100 mouth-watering recipes that showcase the rich culinary traditions of Mexico and offer a variety of flavors and textures to satisfy any palate.

From classic enchiladas to creative twists on the beloved dish, this cookbook has something for everyone. Whether you prefer spicy or mild, meaty or vegetarian, cheesy or light, you'll find a recipe that will delight your taste buds and impress your family and friends.

- Mexican cuisine
- Spicy flavors
- Savory fillings
- Traditional recipes
- Homemade sauces
- Easy-to-follow instructions
- Comfort food
- Family-friendly meals
- Vegetarian options
- Bold and delicious

Each recipe in this cookbook has been carefully crafted to ensure maximum flavor and authenticity. We've included detailed instructions and helpful tips to guide you through the process of making enchiladas from scratch, so even if you're a beginner in the kitchen, you'll be able to create restaurant-quality dishes in no time.

So why not bring a little bit of Mexico to your kitchen and spice up your next fiesta with some delicious enchiladas?

CHEESE ENCHILADAS

1. **Basic Cheese Enchiladas**

12 corn tortillas
3 cups of shredded cheddar cheese
1 can of enchilada sauce
1 diced onion
2 cloves of garlic
Salt and pepper to taste
Preheat the oven to 375°F. In a saucepan, heat the enchilada sauce, onion, and garlic over medium heat. Dip the tortillas in the sauce and place them in a 9x13 inch baking dish. Fill each tortilla with shredded cheese and roll it up. Pour the remaining sauce over the enchiladas and sprinkle with extra cheese. Bake for 25-30 minutes.

2. Creamy Cheese Enchiladas

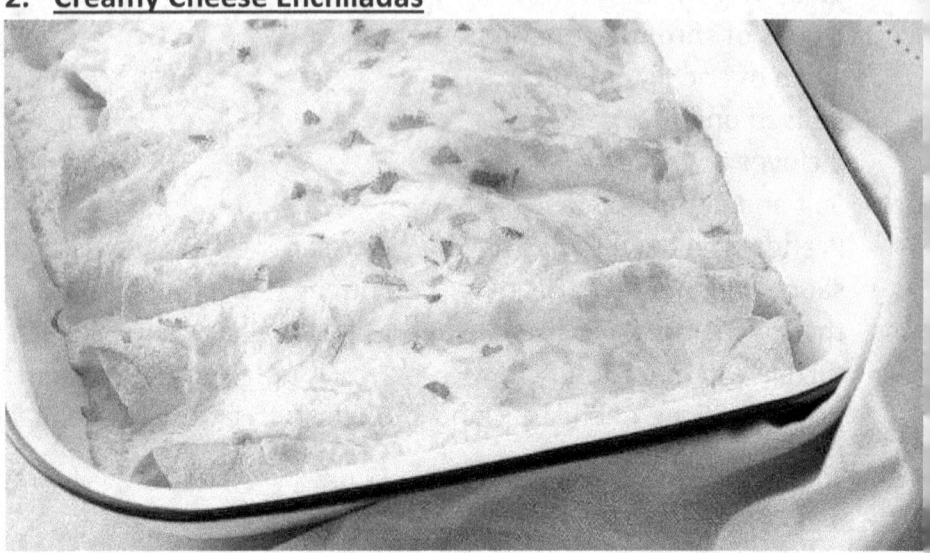

12 corn tortillas
2 cups shredded Monterey Jack cheese
2 tablespoons butter
2 tablespoons flour
2 cups chicken or vegetable broth
1 cup sour cream
Salt and pepper to taste

Preheat oven to 375°F. In a large skillet, melt butter over medium heat. Whisk in flour and cook for 1 minute. Gradually whisk in broth, stirring constantly. Bring to a boil and cook for 2-3 minutes until sauce thickens. Remove from heat and stir in sour cream. Warm tortillas in the microwave for 30 seconds. Fill each tortilla with a handful of cheese. Roll up tightly and place seam-side down in a greased baking dish. Pour the creamy sauce over the top of the enchiladas. Sprinkle with additional cheese. Cover with foil and bake for 20 minutes. Remove foil and bake for an additional 10-15 minutes until cheese is melted and bubbly.

3. Spinach and Cheese Enchiladas

12 corn tortillas
2 cups shredded Monterey Jack cheese
1/4 cup chopped onion
2 cloves garlic, minced
2 tablespoons vegetable oil
1 package (10 ounces) frozen spinach, thawed and drained
1 can (10 ounces) green enchilada sauce
Salt and pepper to taste

Preheat oven to 375°F. In a large skillet, heat oil over medium heat. Add onion and garlic, and cook until onion is soft, about 5 minutes. Add spinach and cook for 1 minute. Remove from heat. Warm tortillas in the microwave for 30 seconds. Fill each tortilla with a handful of cheese and a spoonful of the spinach mixture. Roll up tightly and place seam-side down in a greased baking dish. Pour green enchilada sauce over the top of the enchiladas. Sprinkle with remaining cheese. Cover with foil and bake for 20 minutes. Remove foil and bake for an additional 10-15 minutes until cheese is melted and bubbly.

4. Three-Cheese Enchiladas

12 corn tortillas
1 cup shredded cheddar cheese
1 cup shredded Monterey Jack cheese
1 cup shredded mozzarella cheese
1/4 cup chopped onion
2 cloves garlic, minced
2 tablespoons vegetable oil
1 can (10 ounces) red enchilada sauce
Salt and pepper to taste

Preheat oven to 375°F. In a large skillet, heat oil over medium heat. Add onion and garlic, and cook until onion is soft, about 5 minutes. Add half of the enchilada sauce and stir to combine. Remove from heat. Warm tortillas in the microwave for 30 seconds. Mix the three types of cheese in a bowl. Fill each tortilla with a handful of cheese and a spoonful of the onion mixture. Roll up tightly and place seam-side down in a greased baking dish. Pour remaining enchilada sauce over the top of the enchiladas. Sprinkle with remaining cheese. Cover with foil and bake for 20 minutes. Remove foil and bake for an additional 10-15 minutes until cheese is melted and bubbly.

5. Black Bean and Cheese Enchiladas

12 corn tortillas
2 cups shredded cheddar cheese
1 can (15 ounces) black beans, rinsed and drained
1/4 cup chopped onion
2 cloves garlic, minced
2 tablespoons vegetable oil
1 can (10 ounces) red enchilada sauce
Salt and pepper to taste
Preheat oven to 375°F. In a large skillet, heat oil over medium heat. Add onion and garlic, and cook until onion is soft, about 5 minutes. Add black beans and cook for 1 minute. Remove from heat. Warm tortillas in the microwave for 30 seconds. Fill each tortilla with a handful of cheese and a spoonful of the black bean mixture. Roll up tightly and place seam-side down in a greased baking dish. Pour red enchilada sauce over the top of the enchiladas. Sprinkle with remaining cheese. Cover with foil and bake for 20 minutes. Remove foil and bake for an additional 10-15 minutes until cheese is melted and bubbly.

6. Roasted Vegetable and Cheese Enchiladas

12 corn tortillas
2 cups shredded Monterey Jack cheese
1 red bell pepper, diced
1 green bell pepper, diced
1 zucchini, diced
1 yellow squash, diced
1/4 cup chopped onion
2 cloves garlic, minced
2 tablespoons vegetable oil
1 can (10 ounces) green enchilada sauce
Salt and pepper to taste

Preheat oven to 375°F. Toss diced vegetables in oil and roast on a baking sheet at 400°F for 15-20 minutes until tender. In a large skillet, heat oil over medium heat. Add onion and garlic, and cook until onion is soft, about 5 minutes. Add roasted vegetables and stir to combine. Remove from heat. Warm tortillas in the microwave for 30 seconds. Fill each tortilla with a handful of cheese and a spoonful of the vegetable mixture. Roll up tightly and place seam-side down in a greased baking dish. Pour green enchilada sauce over the top of the enchiladas. Sprinkle with remaining cheese. Cover with foil and bake for 20 minutes. Remove foil and bake for an additional 10-15 minutes until cheese is melted and bubbly.

7. **White Cheese Enchiladas**

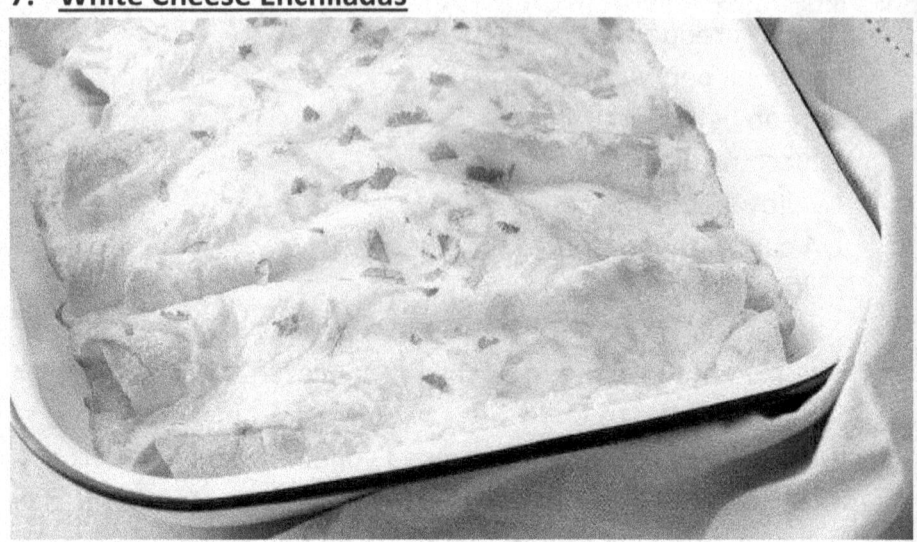

12 flour tortillas
2 cups shredded Monterey Jack cheese
2 tablespoons butter
2 tablespoons flour
2 cups chicken or vegetable broth
1 cup sour cream
1 can (4 ounces) chopped green chilies
Salt and pepper to taste

Preheat oven to 375°F. In a large skillet, melt butter over medium heat. Whisk in flour and cook for 1 minute until bubbly. Gradually whisk in chicken or vegetable broth and bring to a boil. Reduce heat and simmer for 2-3 minutes until thickened. Remove from heat and stir in sour cream and green chilies. Warm tortillas in the microwave for 30 seconds. Fill each tortilla with a handful of cheese. Roll up tightly and place seam-side down in a greased baking dish. Pour white sauce over the top of the enchiladas. Sprinkle with remaining cheese. Cover with foil and bake for 20 minutes. Remove foil and bake for an additional 10-15 minutes until cheese is melted and bubbly.

8. Beef and Cheese Enchiladas

- 12 corn tortillas
- 2 cups shredded cheddar cheese
- 1 pound ground beef
- 1/2 cup chopped onion
- 2 cloves garlic, minced
- 1 can (10 ounces) red enchilada sauce
- Salt and pepper to taste

Preheat oven to 375°F. In a large skillet, cook ground beef over medium heat until browned. Add onion and garlic, and cook until onion is soft, about 5 minutes. Add salt and pepper to taste. Remove from heat. Warm tortillas in the microwave for 30 seconds. Fill each tortilla with a handful of cheese and a spoonful of the beef mixture. Roll up tightly and place seam-side down in a greased baking dish. Pour red enchilada sauce over the top of the enchiladas. Sprinkle with remaining cheese. Cover with foil and bake for 20 minutes. Remove foil and bake for an additional 10-15 minutes until cheese is melted and bubbly.

9. Spinach and Cheese Enchiladas

12 flour tortillas
2 cups shredded Monterey Jack cheese
1 package (10 ounces) frozen spinach, thawed and drained
1/4 cup chopped onion
2 cloves garlic, minced
2 tablespoons butter
2 tablespoons flour
2 cups chicken or vegetable broth
Salt and pepper to taste
Preheat oven to 375°F. In a large skillet, melt butter over medium heat. Whisk in flour and cook for 1 minute. Gradually whisk in broth until smooth. Cook for 5-7 minutes, whisking constantly, until sauce thickens. Remove from heat. Add spinach, onion, and garlic to the skillet and stir to combine. Warm tortillas in the microwave for 30 seconds. Fill each tortilla with a handful of cheese and a spoonful of the spinach mixture. Roll up tightly and place seam-side down in a greased baking dish. Pour white sauce over the top of the enchiladas. Sprinkle with remaining cheese. Cover with foil and bake for 20 minutes. Remove foil and bake for an additional 10-15 minutes until cheese is melted and bubbly.

10. Shrimp and Cheese Enchiladas

12 corn tortillas
2 cups shredded Monterey Jack cheese
1 pound medium shrimp, peeled and deveined
1/4 cup chopped onion
2 cloves garlic, minced
2 tablespoons vegetable oil
1 can (10 ounces) green enchilada sauce
Salt and pepper to taste

Preheat oven to 375°F. In a large skillet, heat oil over medium heat. Add onion and garlic, and cook until onion is soft, about 5 minutes. Add shrimp and cook until pink, about 3-4 minutes. Remove from heat. Warm tortillas in the microwave for 30 seconds. Fill each tortilla with a handful of cheese and a spoonful of the shrimp mixture. Roll up tightly and place seam-side down in a greased baking dish. Pour green enchilada sauce over the top of the enchiladas. Sprinkle with remaining cheese. Cover with foil and bake for 20 minutes. Remove foil and bake for an additional 10-15 minutes until cheese is melted and bubbly.

11. Chicken and Cheese Enchiladas with Verde Sauce

12 corn tortillas
2 cups shredded Monterey Jack cheese
2 cups cooked and shredded chicken
1 can (10 ounces) green enchilada sauce
1/2 cup sour cream
1/4 cup chopped cilantro
Salt and pepper to taste
Preheat oven to 375°F. In a medium bowl, mix together shredded chicken, cilantro, sour cream, salt, and pepper. Warm tortillas in the microwave for 30 seconds. Fill each tortilla with a handful of cheese and a spoonful of the chicken mixture. Roll up tightly and place seam-side down in a greased baking dish. Pour green enchilada sauce over the top of the enchiladas. Sprinkle with remaining cheese. Cover with foil and bake for 20 minutes. Remove foil and bake for an additional 10-15 minutes until cheese is melted and bubbly.

12. Vegetarian Black Bean and Cheese Enchiladas

12 corn tortillas
2 cups shredded Monterey Jack cheese
1 can (15 ounces) black beans, rinsed and drained
1/2 cup frozen corn, thawed
1/4 cup chopped onion
1 can (10 ounces) red enchilada sauce
Salt and pepper to taste
Preheat oven to 375°F. In a medium bowl, mix together black beans, corn, onion, salt, and pepper. Warm tortillas in the microwave for 30 seconds. Fill each tortilla with a handful of cheese and a spoonful of the black bean mixture. Roll up tightly and place seam-side down in a greased baking dish. Pour red enchilada sauce over the top of the enchiladas. Sprinkle with remaining cheese. Cover with foil and bake for 20 minutes. Remove foil and bake for an additional 10-15 minutes until cheese is melted and bubbly.

BEEF ENCHILADAS

13. Basic Beef Enchiladas

1 lb ground beef
12 corn tortillas
1 can of enchilada sauce
1 diced onion
2 cloves of garlic
1 tsp of cumin
Salt and pepper to taste

Preheat the oven to 375°F. In a skillet, cook the beef with onion, garlic, cumin, salt, and pepper until browned. In a saucepan, heat the enchilada sauce over medium heat. Dip the tortillas in the sauce and place them in a 9x13 inch baking dish. Fill each tortilla with the beef mixture and roll it up. Pour the remaining sauce over the enchiladas and bake for 25-30 minutes.

14. Beef and Bean Enchiladas

1 lb ground beef
1 can of black beans, drained and rinsed
1 diced onion
2 cloves of garlic
1 can of red enchilada sauce
12 corn tortillas
Salt and pepper to taste
Preheat the oven to 375°F. In a skillet, cook the beef with onion, garlic, salt, and pepper until browned. Add the black beans and mix well. In a saucepan, heat the enchilada sauce over medium heat. Dip the tortillas in the sauce and place them in a 9x13 inch baking dish. Fill each tortilla with the beef and bean mixture and roll it up. Pour the remaining sauce over the enchiladas and bake for 25-30 minutes.

15. Spicy Beef Enchiladas

12 flour tortillas
2 cups shredded pepper jack cheese
1 pound ground beef
1 can (10 ounces) enchilada sauce
1 can (4 ounces) diced green chilies, drained
1 tablespoon chili powder
1/2 teaspoon cumin
Salt and pepper to taste

Preheat oven to 375°F. In a large skillet, cook ground beef over medium heat until beef is browned and cooked through. Drain any excess fat. Add chili powder, cumin, salt, and pepper to taste. Stir in diced green chilies. Warm tortillas in the microwave for 30 seconds. Fill each tortilla with a handful of cheese and a spoonful of the beef mixture. Roll up tightly and place seam-side down in a greased baking dish. Pour enchilada sauce over the top of the enchiladas. Sprinkle with remaining cheese. Cover with foil and bake for 20 minutes. Remove foil and bake for an additional 10-15 minutes until cheese is melted and bubbly.

16. Beef Enchiladas with Homemade Sauce

- 12 corn tortillas
- 2 cups shredded cheddar cheese
- 1 pound ground beef
- 1/2 cup chopped onion
- 2 cloves garlic, minced
- 1 can (14.5 ounces) diced tomatoes
- 1 tablespoon chili powder
- 1 teaspoon cumin
- 1 teaspoon paprika
- 1/2 teaspoon oregano
- Salt and pepper to taste

Preheat oven to 375°F. In a large skillet, cook ground beef and onion over medium heat until beef is browned and cooked through. Drain any excess fat. Add garlic and cook for 1 minute. Add diced tomatoes, chili powder, cumin, paprika, oregano, salt, and pepper to taste. Bring to a simmer and cook for 10-15 minutes, stirring occasionally. Warm tortillas in the microwave for 30 seconds. Fill each tortilla with a handful of cheese and a spoonful of the beef mixture. Roll up tightly and place seam-side down in a greased baking dish. Pour homemade enchilada sauce over the top of the enchiladas. Sprinkle with remaining cheese. Cover with foil and bake for 20 minutes. Remove foil and bake for an additional 10-15 minutes until cheese is melted and bubbly.

17. Beef Enchiladas with Green Sauce

- 12 flour tortillas
- 2 cups shredded Monterey Jack cheese
- 1 pound ground beef
- 1 can (10 ounces) green enchilada sauce
- 1 can (4 ounces) diced green chilies, drained
- 1/2 teaspoon cumin
- Salt and pepper to taste

Preheat oven to 375°F. In a large skillet, cook ground beef over medium heat until beef is browned and cooked through. Drain any excess fat. Add diced green chilies, cumin, salt, and pepper to taste. Warm tortillas in the microwave for 30 seconds. Fill each tortilla with a handful of cheese and a spoonful of the beef mixture. Roll up tightly and place seam-side down in a greased baking dish. Pour green enchilada sauce over the top of the enchiladas. Sprinkle with remaining cheese. Cover with foil and bake for 20 minutes. Remove foil and bake for an additional 10-15 minutes until cheese is melted and bubbly.

18. Slow Cooker Beef Enchiladas

12 flour tortillas
2 cups shredded cheddar cheese
2 pounds beef chuck roast
1 can (10 ounces) enchilada sauce
1 can (4 ounces) diced green chilies, drained
1 tablespoon chili powder
1/2 teaspoon cumin
Salt and pepper to taste

Place beef chuck roast in a slow cooker. Add enchilada sauce, diced green chilies, chili powder, cumin, salt, and pepper to taste. Cover and cook on low for 8-10 hours or until beef is tender and falls apart easily. Shred beef with a fork. Preheat oven to 375°F. Warm tortillas in the microwave for 30 seconds. Fill each tortilla with a handful of cheese and a spoonful of the shredded beef. Roll up tightly and place seam-side down in a greased baking dish. Pour remaining sauce from the slow cooker over the top of the enchiladas. Sprinkle with remaining cheese. Cover with foil and bake for 20 minutes. Remove foil and bake for an additional 10-15 minutes until cheese is melted and bubbly.

19. Beef Enchiladas with Creamy Sauce

12 flour tortillas
2 cups shredded Monterey Jack cheese
1 pound ground beef
1 can (10 ounces) red enchilada sauce
1 can (10.75 ounces) cream of mushroom soup
1/2 cup sour cream
Salt and pepper to taste

Preheat oven to 375°F. In a large skillet, cook ground beef over medium heat until beef is browned and cooked through. Drain any excess fat. Add salt and pepper to taste.

In a separate bowl, mix together red enchilada sauce, cream of mushroom soup, and sour cream until well combined. Warm tortillas in the microwave for 30 seconds. Fill each tortilla with a handful of cheese and a spoonful of the beef mixture. Roll up tightly and place seam-side down in a greased baking dish. Pour creamy sauce over the top of the enchiladas. Sprinkle with remaining cheese. Cover with foil and bake for 20 minutes. Remove foil and bake for an additional 10-15 minutes until cheese is melted and bubbly.

20. Beef Enchiladas with Mole Sauce

12 flour tortillas
2 cups shredded Monterey Jack cheese
1 pound ground beef
1 can (10 ounces) red enchilada sauce
1/4 cup mole sauce
Salt and pepper to taste
Preheat oven to 375°F. In a large skillet, cook ground beef over medium heat until beef is browned and cooked through. Drain any excess fat. Add salt and pepper to taste. Warm tortillas in the microwave for 30 seconds. Fill each tortilla with a handful of cheese and a spoonful of the beef mixture. Roll up tightly and place seam-side down in a greased baking dish. In a separate bowl, mix together red enchilada sauce and mole sauce until well combined. Pour sauce over the top of the enchiladas. Sprinkle with remaining cheese. Cover with foil and bake for 20 minutes. Remove foil and bake for an additional 10-15 minutes until cheese is melted and bubbly.

21. Beef Enchiladas with Chipotle Sauce

12 flour tortillas
2 cups shredded cheddar cheese
1 pound ground beef
1 can (10 ounces) red enchilada sauce
1 can (7 ounces) chipotle peppers in adobo sauce, chopped
Salt and pepper to taste

Preheat oven to 375°F. In a large skillet, cook ground beef over medium heat until beef is browned and cooked through. Drain any excess fat. Add salt and pepper to taste. Warm tortillas in the microwave for 30 seconds. Fill each tortilla with a handful of cheese and a spoonful of the beef mixture. Roll up tightly and place seam-side down in a greased baking dish. In a separate bowl, mix together red enchilada sauce and chopped chipotle peppers in adobo sauce until well combined. Pour sauce over the top of the enchiladas. Sprinkle with remaining cheese. Cover with foil and bake for 20 minutes. Remove foil and bake for an additional 10-15 minutes until cheese is melted and bubbly.

22. Beef Enchiladas with Tomatillo Sauce

12 flour tortillas
2 cups shredded Monterey Jack cheese
1 pound ground beef
1 can (10 ounces) red enchilada sauce
1 can (11 ounces) tomatillos, drained and chopped
1/4 cup chopped cilantro
Salt and pepper to taste

Preheat oven to 375°F. In a large skillet, cook ground beef over medium heat until beef is browned and cooked through. Drain any excess fat. Add chopped tomatillos, cilantro, salt, and pepper to taste. Warm tortillas in the microwave for 30 seconds. Fill each tortilla with a handful of cheese and a spoonful of the beef mixture. Roll up tightly and place seam-side down in a greased baking dish. In a separate bowl, mix together red enchilada sauce and chopped tomatillos until well combined. Pour sauce over the top of the enchiladas. Sprinkle with remaining cheese. Cover with foil and bake for 20 minutes. Remove foil and bake for an additional 10-15 minutes until cheese is melted and bubbly.

23. Beef Enchiladas with Ranchero Sauce

12 flour tortillas
2 cups shredded cheddar cheese
1 pound ground beef
1 can (10 ounces) red enchilada sauce
1 can (14.5 ounces) diced tomatoes, drained
1/4 cup chopped onion
1 tablespoon chopped garlic
Salt and pepper to taste
Preheat oven to 375°F. In a large skillet, cook ground beef over medium heat until beef is browned and cooked through. Drain any excess fat. Add diced tomatoes, chopped onion, chopped garlic, salt, and pepper to taste. Warm tortillas in the microwave for 30 seconds. Fill each tortilla with a handful of cheese and a spoonful of the beef mixture. Roll up tightly and place seam-side down in a greased baking dish. In a separate bowl, mix together red enchilada sauce and diced tomatoes until well combined. Pour sauce over the top of the enchiladas. Sprinkle with remaining cheese. Cover with foil and bake for 20 minutes. Remove foil and bake for an additional 10-15 minutes until cheese is melted and bubbly.

24. Beef Enchiladas with Green Chile Sauce

- 12 flour tortillas
- 2 cups shredded Monterey Jack cheese
- 1 pound ground beef
- 1 can (10 ounces) red enchilada sauce
- 1 can (4 ounces) chopped green chiles
- Salt and pepper to taste

Preheat oven to 375°F. In a large skillet, cook ground beef over medium heat until beef is browned and cooked through. Drain any excess fat. Add chopped green chiles, salt, and pepper to taste. Warm tortillas in the microwave for 30 seconds. Fill each tortilla with a handful of cheese and a spoonful of the beef mixture. Roll up tightly and place seam-side down in a greased baking dish. In a separate bowl, mix together red enchilada sauce and chopped green chiles until well combined. Pour sauce over the top of the enchiladas. Sprinkle with remaining cheese. Cover with foil and bake for 20 minutes. Remove foil and bake for an additional 10-15 minutes until cheese is melted and bubbly

.

25. Beef Enchiladas with Salsa Verde

12 flour tortillas
2 cups shredded cheddar cheese
1 pound ground beef
1 jar (16 ounces) salsa verde
Salt and pepper to taste

Preheat oven to 375°F. In a large skillet, cook ground beef over medium heat until beef is browned and cooked through. Drain any excess fat. Add salt and pepper to taste. Warm tortillas in the microwave for 30 seconds. Fill each tortilla with a handful of cheese and a spoonful of the beef mixture. Roll up tightly and place seam-side down in a greased baking dish. Pour salsa verde over the top of the enchiladas. Sprinkle with remaining cheese. Cover with foil and bake for 20 minutes. Remove foil and bake for an additional 10-15 minutes until cheese is melted and bubbly.

26. Beef Enchiladas with Pico de Gallo

12 flour tortillas
2 cups
shredded Monterey Jack cheese
1 pound ground beef
1 can (10 ounces) red enchilada sauce
1 cup homemade or store-bought pico de gallo

Preheat oven to 375°F. In a large skillet, cook ground beef over medium heat until beef is browned and cooked through. Drain any excess fat. Warm tortillas in the microwave for 30 seconds. Fill each tortilla with a handful of cheese and a spoonful of the beef mixture. Roll up tightly and place seam-side down in a greased baking dish. Pour enchilada sauce over the top of the enchiladas. Spoon pico de gallo on top of the enchilada sauce. Sprinkle with remaining cheese. Cover with foil and bake for 20 minutes. Remove foil and bake for an additional 10-15 minutes until cheese is melted and bubbly.

27. Beef Enchiladas with Mole Sauce

12 flour tortillas
2 cups shredded cheddar cheese
1 pound ground beef
1 can (10 ounces) red enchilada sauce
1/2 cup homemade or store-bought mole sauce

Preheat oven to 375°F. In a large skillet, cook ground beef over medium heat until beef is browned and cooked through. Drain any excess fat. Warm tortillas in the microwave for 30 seconds. Fill each tortilla with a handful of cheese and a spoonful of the beef mixture. Roll up tightly and place seam-side down in a greased baking dish. Pour enchilada sauce over the top of the enchiladas. Spoon mole sauce on top of the enchilada sauce. Sprinkle with remaining cheese. Cover with foil and bake for 20 minutes. Remove foil and bake for an additional 10-15 minutes until cheese is melted and bubbly.

28. Beef Enchiladas with Chipotle Sauce

12 flour tortillas
2 cups shredded Monterey Jack cheese
1 pound ground beef
1 can (10 ounces) red enchilada sauce
2 tablespoons chipotle peppers in adobo sauce, chopped

Preheat oven to 375°F. In a large skillet, cook ground beef over medium heat until beef is browned and cooked through. Drain any excess fat. Warm tortillas in the microwave for 30 seconds. Fill each tortilla with a handful of cheese and a spoonful of the beef mixture. Roll up tightly and place seam-side down in a greased baking dish. In a separate bowl, mix together red enchilada sauce and chopped chipotle peppers until well combined. Pour sauce over the top of the enchiladas. Sprinkle with remaining cheese. Cover with foil and bake for 20 minutes. Remove foil and bake for an additional 10-15 minutes until cheese is melted and bubbly.

CHICKEN ENCHILADAS

29. Basic Chicken Enchiladas

1 lb cooked and shredded chicken
12 corn tortillas
1 can of green enchilada sauce
1 diced onion
2 cloves of garlic
1 tsp of cumin
Salt and pepper to taste
Preheat the oven to 375°F. In a saucepan, heat the enchilada sauce, onion, garlic, cumin, salt, and pepper over medium heat. Dip the tortillas in the sauce and place them in a 9x13 inch baking dish. Fill each tortilla with the chicken and roll it up. Pour the remaining sauce over the enchiladas and bake for 25-30 minutes.

30. Chicken and Spinach Enchiladas

- 1 lb cooked and shredded chicken
- 2 cups of fresh spinach, chopped
- 1 diced onion
- 2 cloves of garlic
- 1 can of green enchilada sauce
- 12 corn tortillas
- Salt and pepper to taste

Preheat the oven to 375°F. In a skillet, cook the onion and garlic until softened. Add the spinach and cook until wilted. Add the shredded chicken and season with salt and pepper. In a saucepan, heat the enchilada sauce over medium heat. Dip the tortillas in the sauce and place them in a 9x13 inch baking dish. Fill each tortilla with the chicken and spinach mixture and roll it up. Pour the remaining sauce over the enchiladas and bake for 25-30 minutes.

31. Green Chile Chicken Enchiladas

Ingredients:

2 lbs. boneless, skinless chicken breasts
1 can (14 oz.) green enchilada sauce
1 can (4 oz.) diced green chiles
2 cups shredded Monterey Jack cheese
10-12 corn tortillas
Salt and pepper, to taste

Instructions:

Preheat the oven to 375°F.
Season chicken with salt and pepper, then cook in a large skillet over medium-high heat until browned and cooked through. Shred the chicken and set aside.
In a large bowl, mix together the green enchilada sauce and diced green chiles.
In a separate bowl, mix together the shredded chicken and 1 cup of shredded cheese.
Warm the tortillas in the microwave or on a griddle until they are soft and pliable.
Place a generous spoonful of the chicken mixture onto each tortilla and roll up tightly.
Place the rolled up tortillas seam-side down in a 9x13 inch baking dish.
Pour the green sauce mixture over the top of the enchiladas and sprinkle with the remaining shredded cheese.
Bake in the preheated oven for 20-25 minutes, or until the cheese is melted and bubbly.

32. Creamy Chicken Enchiladas

Ingredients:

2 lbs. boneless, skinless chicken breasts
1 can (10 oz.) cream of chicken soup
1 can (4 oz.) diced green chiles
1/2 cup sour cream
2 cups shredded Monterey Jack cheese
10-12 flour tortillas
Salt and pepper, to taste

Instructions:

Preheat the oven to 375°F.
Season chicken with salt and pepper, then cook in a large skillet over medium-high heat until browned and cooked through.
Shred the chicken and set aside.
In a large bowl, mix together the cream of chicken soup, diced green chiles, and sour cream.
In a separate bowl, mix together the shredded chicken and 1 cup of shredded cheese.
6. Warm the tortillas in the microwave or on a griddle until they are soft and pliable.

Place a generous spoonful of the chicken mixture onto each tortilla and roll up tightly.
Place the rolled up tortillas seam-side down in a 9x13 inch baking dish.
Pour the creamy sauce mixture over the top of the enchiladas and sprinkle with the remaining shredded cheese.
Bake in the preheated oven for 20-25 minutes, or until the cheese is melted and bubbly.

33. Red Chile Chicken Enchiladas

Ingredients:

2 lbs. boneless, skinless chicken breasts
2 cups red enchilada sauce
1 can (4 oz.) diced green chiles
2 cups shredded cheddar cheese
10-12 corn tortillas
Salt and pepper, to taste

Instructions:

Preheat the oven to 375°F.
Season chicken with salt and pepper, then cook in a large skillet over medium-high heat until browned and cooked through. Shred the chicken and set aside.
In a large bowl, mix together the red enchilada sauce and diced green chiles.
In a separate bowl, mix together the shredded chicken and 1 cup of shredded cheese.
Warm the tortillas in the microwave or on a griddle until they are soft and pliable.
Place a generous spoonful of the chicken mixture onto each tortilla and roll up tightly.
Place the rolled up tortillas seam-side down in a 9x13 inch baking dish.
Pour the red sauce mixture over the top of the enchiladas and sprinkle with the remaining shredded cheese.
Bake in the preheated oven for 20-25 minutes, or until the cheese is melted and bubbly.

34. Spicy Chicken Enchiladas

Ingredients:

2 lbs. boneless, skinless chicken breasts
1 can (10 oz.) diced tomatoes and green chilies
1 can (4 oz.) diced jalapeños
2 cups shredded pepper jack cheese
10-12 corn tortillas
Salt and pepper, to taste

Instructions:

Preheat the oven to 375°F.
Season chicken with salt and pepper, then cook in a large skillet over medium-high heat until browned and cooked through. Shred the chicken and set aside.
In a large bowl, mix together the diced tomatoes and green chilies, and diced jalapeños.
In a separate bowl, mix together the shredded chicken and 1 cup of shredded cheese.
Warm the tortillas in the microwave or on a griddle until they are soft and pliable.
Place a generous spoonful of the chicken mixture onto each tortilla and roll up tightly.
Place the rolled up tortillas seam-side down in a 9x13 inch baking dish.
Pour the tomato and jalapeño mixture over the top of the enchiladas and sprinkle with the remaining shredded cheese.
Bake in the preheated oven for 20-25 minutes, or until the cheese is melted and bubbly.

35. Cheesy Chicken Enchiladas

Ingredients:

2 lbs. boneless, skinless chicken breasts
2 cups shredded cheddar cheese
1 can (4 oz.) diced green chiles
1/2 cup salsa
10-12 flour tortillas
Salt and pepper, to taste

Instructions:

Preheat the oven to 375°F.
Season chicken with salt and pepper, then cook in a large skillet over medium-high heat until browned and cooked through.
Shred the chicken and set aside.
In a large bowl, mix together the shredded cheese, diced green chiles, and salsa.
In a separate bowl, mix together the shredded chicken.
Warm the tortillas in the microwave or on a griddle until they are soft and pliable.
Place a generous spoonful of the chicken mixture onto each tortilla and roll up tightly.
Place the rolled up tortillas seam-side down in a 9x13 inch baking dish.
Pour the cheese mixture over the top of the enchiladas.
Bake in the preheated oven for 20-25 minutes, or until the cheese is melted and bubbly.

36. Creamy Chicken Enchiladas with Poblano Sauce

Ingredients:

2 lbs. boneless, skinless chicken breasts
1/2 cup heavy cream
1/4 cup sour cream
1 can (4 oz.) diced green chiles
2 cups shredded Monterey jack cheese
10-12 corn tortillas
Salt and pepper, to taste

Poblano Sauce:

2 large poblano peppers
1/2 onion, chopped
2 cloves garlic, minced
1/2 cup chicken broth
1/2 cup heavy cream
Salt and pepper, to taste

Instructions:

Preheat the oven to 375°F.
Season chicken with salt and pepper, then cook in a large skillet over medium-high heat until browned and cooked through. Shred the chicken and set aside.
In a large bowl, mix together the heavy cream, sour cream, diced green chiles, and 1 cup of shredded Monterey jack cheese.
In a separate bowl, mix together the shredded chicken.
Warm the tortillas in the microwave or on a griddle until they are soft and pliable.
Place a generous spoonful of the chicken mixture onto each tortilla and roll up tightly.
Place the rolled up tortillas seam-side down in a 9x13 inch baking dish.
Pour the creamy sauce mixture over the top of the enchiladas and sprinkle with the remaining shredded cheese.
Bake in the preheated oven for 20-25 minutes, or until the cheese is melted and bubbly.

For the Poblano Sauce:

Roast the poblano peppers over an open flame or under the broiler until the skin is charred and blistered.
Remove from heat and place in a plastic bag for 10-15 minutes to steam.
Remove the skin, stem, and seeds from the peppers and chop the flesh.
In a large saucepan, sauté the onion and garlic until softened.
Add the chopped poblanos, chicken broth, and heavy cream to the saucepan and simmer for 10-15 minutes.
Season with salt and pepper to taste.
Pour the sauce over the enchiladas before serving.

37. Chicken Enchiladas with Verde Sauce

Ingredients:

2 lbs. boneless, skinless chicken breasts
2 cups shredded Monterey jack cheese
1 can (4 oz.) diced green chiles
1 jar (16 oz.) salsa verde
10-12 corn tortillas
Salt and pepper, to taste

Instructions:

Preheat the oven to 375°F.
2. Season chicken with salt and pepper, then cook in a large skillet over medium-high heat until browned and cooked through.

Shred the chicken and set aside.
In a large bowl, mix together the shredded cheese, diced green chiles, and 1/2 cup of salsa verde.
In a separate bowl, mix together the shredded chicken.
Warm the tortillas in the microwave or on a griddle until they are soft and pliable.
Place a generous spoonful of the chicken mixture onto each tortilla and roll up tightly.
Place the rolled up tortillas seam-side down in a 9x13 inch baking dish.
Pour the remaining salsa verde over the top of the enchiladas.
Bake in the preheated oven for 20-25 minutes, or until the cheese is melted and bubbly.

38. Creamy Chicken Enchiladas with Tomatillo Sauce

Ingredients:

2 lbs. boneless, skinless chicken breasts
1/2 cup heavy cream
1/4 cup sour cream
1 can (4 oz.) diced green chiles
2 cups shredded Monterey jack cheese
10-12 corn tortillas
Salt and pepper, to taste

Tomatillo Sauce:

8 tomatillos, husked and rinsed
1/2 onion, chopped
2 cloves garlic, minced
1/2 cup chicken broth
1/2 cup heavy cream
Salt and pepper, to taste

Instructions:

Preheat the oven to 375°F.
Season chicken with salt and pepper, then cook in a large skillet over medium-high heat until browned and cooked through.
Shred the chicken and set aside.
In a large bowl, mix together the heavy cream, sour cream, diced green chiles, and 1 cup of shredded Monterey jack cheese.
In a separate bowl, mix together the shredded chicken.
Warm the tortillas in the microwave or on a griddle until they are soft and pliable.
Place a generous spoonful of the chicken mixture onto each tortilla and roll up tightly.
Place the rolled up tortillas seam-side down in a 9x13 inch baking dish.
Pour the creamy sauce mixture over the top of the enchiladas and sprinkle with the remaining shredded cheese.
Bake in the preheated oven for 20-25 minutes, or until the cheese is melted and bubbly.

For the Tomatillo Sauce:

Preheat the broiler.
Place the tomatillos on a baking sheet and broil for 5-7 minutes, or until the skin is charred and blistered.
Remove from heat and let cool.
In a blender or food processor, puree the tomatillos, onion, garlic, chicken broth, and heavy cream until smooth.
Season with salt and pepper to taste.
Pour the sauce over the enchiladas before serving.

FISH AND SEAFOOD

39. Shrimp Enchiladas

1 lb cooked and chopped shrimp
12 corn tortillas
1 can of red enchilada sauce
1 diced onion
2 cloves of garlic
1 tsp of cumin
Salt and pepper to taste
Preheat the oven to 375°F. In a saucepan, heat the enchilada sauce, onion, garlic, cumin, salt, and pepper over medium heat. Dip the tortillas in the sauce and place them in a 9x13 inch baking dish. Fill each tortilla with the shrimp and roll it up. Pour the remaining sauce over the enchiladas and bake for 25-30 minutes.

40. Crab Enchiladas

Ingredients:

- 1 lb. crabmeat, picked over for shells
- 2 cups shredded Monterey jack cheese
- 1 can (4 oz.) diced green chiles
- 1 jar (16 oz.) salsa
- 10-12 corn tortillas
- Salt and pepper, to taste

Instructions:

Preheat the oven to 375°F.
In a large bowl, mix together the crabmeat, shredded cheese, diced green chiles, and 1/2 cup of salsa.
Warm the tortillas in the microwave or on a griddle until they are soft and pliable.
Place a generous spoonful of the crabmeat mixture onto each tortilla and roll up tightly.
Place the rolled up tortillas seam-side down in a 9x13 inch baking dish.
Pour the remaining salsa over the top of the enchiladas.
Bake in the preheated oven for 20-25 minutes, or until the cheese is melted and bubbly.

41. Seafood Enchiladas

Ingredients:
1 lb. cooked shrimp, peeled and deveined
1 lb. cooked crab meat, shredded
1 can (4 oz.) diced green chiles
1/2 cup chopped onion
2 cloves garlic, minced
1 tsp. ground cumin
1 tsp. chili powder
1 tsp. dried oregano
1 can (10 oz.) enchilada sauce
10-12 corn tortillas
1 cup shredded Monterey jack cheese
1/4 cup chopped fresh cilantro
Salt and pepper, to taste
Optional toppings: diced avocado, sliced jalapenos, sour cream, lime wedges

Instructions:

Preheat the oven to 375°F.
In a large bowl, mix together the cooked shrimp, cooked crab meat, diced green chiles, chopped onion, minced garlic, cumin, chili powder, and oregano. Season with salt and pepper to taste.
Warm the tortillas in the microwave or on a griddle until they are soft and pliable.
Spread a small amount of enchilada sauce in the bottom of a 9x13 inch baking dish.
Place a generous spoonful of the seafood mixture onto each tortilla and roll up tightly.
Place the rolled up tortillas seam-side down in the baking dish.
Pour the remaining enchilada sauce over the top of the enchiladas.
Sprinkle the shredded cheese over the top of the enchiladas.
Bake in the preheated oven for 20-25 minutes, or until the cheese is melted and bubbly.
Sprinkle the chopped cilantro over the top of the enchiladas.
Serve hot with optional toppings if desired.

42. Salmon Enchiladas

Ingredients:

1 lb. cooked salmon, flaked
1 can (4 oz.) diced green chiles
1/2 cup chopped red onion
2 cloves garlic, minced
1 tsp. ground cumin
1 tsp. chili powder
Salt and pepper, to taste
10-12 corn tortillas
1 can (10 oz.) enchilada sauce
1 cup shredded Monterey jack cheese
Fresh cilantro, chopped

Instructions:

Preheat the oven to 375°F.
In a large bowl, mix together the flaked salmon, diced green chiles, chopped red onion, minced garlic, cumin, chili powder, and salt and pepper to taste.
Warm the tortillas in the microwave or on a griddle until they are soft and pliable.
Spread a small amount of enchilada sauce in the bottom of a 9x13 inch baking dish.
Place a generous spoonful of the salmon mixture onto each tortilla and roll up tightly.
Place the rolled up tortillas seam-side down in the baking dish.
Pour the remaining enchilada sauce over the top of the enchiladas.
Sprinkle the shredded cheese over the top of the enchiladas.
Bake in the preheated oven for 20-25 minutes, or until the cheese is melted and bubbly.
Garnish with fresh cilantro and serve hot.

43. Grilled Fish Enchiladas

Ingredients:

- 1 lb. white fish fillets, such as tilapia or cod
- 1 red onion, sliced
- 1 red bell pepper, sliced
- 1 yellow bell pepper, sliced
- 1 tsp. chili powder
- 1 tsp. ground cumin
- Salt and pepper, to taste
- 10-12 corn tortillas
- 1 can (10 oz.) enchilada sauce
- 1 cup shredded Monterey jack cheese
- Fresh cilantro, chopped

Instructions:

Preheat a grill or grill pan to medium-high heat.

Season the fish fillets with chili powder, cumin, salt, and pepper.

Grill the fish for 5-6 minutes per side, or until cooked through.

Remove the fish from the grill and let it cool slightly. Flake the fish into small pieces.

In a large bowl, mix together the flaked fish, sliced red onion, sliced red bell pepper, and sliced yellow bell pepper.

Warm the tortillas in the microwave or on a griddle until they are soft and pliable.

Spread a small amount of enchilada sauce in the bottom of a 9x13 inch baking dish.

Place a generous spoonful of the fish mixture onto each tortilla and roll up tightly.

Place the rolled up tortillas seam-side down in the baking dish.

Pour the remaining enchilada sauce over the top of the enchiladas.

Sprinkle the shredded cheese over the top of the enchiladas.

Bake in a preheated oven at 375°F for 20-25 minutes, or until the cheese is melted and bubbly.

Garnish with fresh cilantro and serve hot.

44. Tuna Enchiladas

Ingredients:

2 cans (5 oz. each) canned tuna, drained
1 can (4 oz.) diced green chiles
1/2 cup chopped red onion
2 continue
cloves garlic, minced
1 tsp. ground cumin
1 tsp. chili powder
Salt and pepper, to taste
10-12 corn tortillas
1 can (10 oz.) enchilada sauce
1 cup shredded cheddar cheese
Fresh cilantro, chopped

Instructions:

Preheat the oven to 375°F.
In a large bowl, mix together the canned tuna, diced green chiles, chopped red onion, minced garlic, cumin, chili powder, and salt and pepper to taste.
Warm the tortillas in the microwave or on a griddle until they are soft and pliable.
Spread a small amount of enchilada sauce in the bottom of a 9x13 inch baking dish.
Place a generous spoonful of the tuna mixture onto each tortilla and roll up tightly.
Place the rolled up tortillas seam-side down in the baking dish.
Pour the remaining enchilada sauce over the top of the enchiladas.
Sprinkle the shredded cheese over the top of the enchiladas.
Bake in the preheated oven for 20-25 minutes, or until the cheese is melted and bubbly.
Garnish with fresh cilantro and serve hot.

45. Mahi-Mahi Enchiladas

Ingredients:

1 lb. mahi-mahi fillets, skin removed
1 red onion, diced
1 red bell pepper, diced
1 green bell pepper, diced
2 cloves garlic, minced
1 tsp. ground cumin
1 tsp. chili powder
Salt and pepper, to taste
10-12 corn tortillas
1 can (10 oz.) red enchilada sauce
1 cup shredded cheddar cheese
Fresh cilantro, chopped

Instructions:
1. Preheat the oven to 375°F.
2. Season the mahi-mahi fillets with cumin, chili powder, salt, and pepper.

Heat a large skillet over medium-high heat and cook the mahi-mahi fillets for 3-4 minutes per side, or until cooked through. Remove the mahi-mahi from the skillet and set aside to cool.
In the same skillet, sauté the diced red onion, red bell pepper, green bell pepper, and minced garlic for 3-4 minutes, or until tender.
Flake the cooked mahi-mahi into small pieces and add it to the skillet with the vegetables.
Warm the tortillas in the microwave or on a griddle until they are soft and pliable.
Spread a small amount of red enchilada sauce in the bottom of a 9x13 inch baking dish.
Place a generous spoonful of the mahi-mahi and vegetable mixture onto each tortilla and roll up tightly.
Place the rolled up tortillas seam-side down in the baking dish.
Pour the remaining red enchilada sauce over the top of the enchiladas.
Sprinkle the shredded cheese over the top of the enchiladas.
Bake in the preheated oven for 20-25 minutes, or until the cheese is melted and bubbly.
Garnish with fresh cilantro and serve hot.

VEGETABLE ENCHILADAS

46. Vegetarian Enchiladas

1 can of black beans, drained and rinsed
1 can of corn, drained
1 diced onion
2 cloves of garlic
1 can of green enchilada sauce
12 corn tortillas
Salt and pepper to taste

Preheat the oven to 375°F. In a skillet, cook the onion and garlic until softened. Add the black beans and corn, and season with salt and pepper. In a saucepan, heat the enchilada sauce over medium heat. Dip the tortillas in the sauce and place them in a 9x13 inch baking dish. Fill each tortilla with the bean and corn mixture and roll it up. Pour the remaining sauce over the enchiladas and bake for 25-30 minutes.

47. Spinach and Mushroom Enchiladas

2 cups of fresh spinach, chopped
1 cup of sliced mushrooms
1 diced onion
2 cloves of garlic
1 can of red enchilada sauce
12 corn tortillas
Salt and pepper to taste
Preheat the oven to 375°F. In a skillet, cook the onion and garlic until softened. Add the mushrooms and spinach, and season with salt and pepper. In a saucepan, heat the enchilada sauce over medium heat. Dip the tortillas in the sauce and place them in a 9x13 inch baking dish. Fill each tortilla with the spinach and mushroom mixture and roll it up. Pour the remaining sauce over the enchiladas and bake for 25-30 minutes.

48. Sweet Potato and Black Bean Enchiladas

Ingredients:
1 large sweet potato, peeled and diced
1 onion, chopped
1 can (15 oz) black beans, drained and rinsed
1 can (10 oz) enchilada sauce
8-10 corn tortillas
1 cup shredded cheddar cheese
Salt and pepper, to taste

Instructions:
Preheat oven to 350°F.
In a large skillet, cook the sweet potato and onion over medium heat until tender.
Add the black beans to the skillet and stir to combine.
Stir in the enchilada sauce, and season with salt and pepper to taste.
Spread a small amount of the sweet potato and black bean mixture onto each tortilla and roll up tightly.
Place the rolled-up tortillas seam-side down in a 9x13 inch baking dish.
Pour the remaining sweet potato and black bean mixture over the tortillas, and sprinkle with shredded cheese.
Bake for 20-25 minutes, until cheese is melted and bubbly.

49. Roasted Vegetable Enchiladas

Ingredients:

- 2 red bell peppers, sliced
- 2 yellow squash, sliced
- 1 zucchini, sliced
- 1 onion, sliced
- 2 tbsp olive oil
- Salt and pepper, to taste
- 8-10 corn tortillas
- 1 can (15 oz) black beans, drained and rinsed
- 1 1/2 cups shredded cheddar cheese
- 1 can (15 oz) enchilada sauce

Instructions:

Preheat the oven to 400°F.

Toss the sliced bell peppers, yellow squash, zucchini, and onion in olive oil and season with salt and pepper.

Spread the vegetables out on a baking sheet and roast in the preheated oven for 20-25 minutes or until tender and lightly browned.

Warm the corn tortillas in the microwave or on a griddle until they are soft and pliable.

Pour a small amount of enchilada sauce in the bottom of a 9x13 inch baking dish.

Place a spoonful of the roasted vegetables and black beans onto each tortilla and roll up tightly.

Place the rolled up tortillas seam-side down in the baking dish.

Pour the remaining enchilada sauce over the top of the enchiladas.

Sprinkle the shredded cheddar cheese over the top of the enchiladas.

Bake in the preheated oven for 20-25 minutes, or until the cheese is melted and bubbly.

Garnish with fresh cilantro and serve hot.

50. Cauliflower Enchiladas

Ingredients:

- 1 head of cauliflower, chopped into small florets
- 1 onion, chopped
- 2 garlic cloves, minced
- 1 can (15 oz) black beans, drained and rinsed
- 1 tsp ground cumin
- 1 tsp chili powder
- Salt and pepper, to taste
- 8-10 corn tortillas
- 1 1/2 cups shredded cheddar cheese
- 1 can (15 oz) enchilada sauce

Instructions:

Preheat the oven to 350°F.

In a large skillet, sauté the chopped onion and garlic until fragrant, about 2-3 minutes.

Add the chopped cauliflower to the skillet and cook until tender, about 10-12 minutes.

Add the black beans, cumin, chili powder, salt, and pepper to the skillet and stir until well combined.

Warm the corn tortillas in the microwave or on a griddle until they are soft and pliable.

Pour a small amount of enchilada sauce in the bottom of a 9x13 inch baking dish.

Place a generous spoonful of the cauliflower and black bean mixture onto each tortilla and roll up tightly.

Place the rolled up tortillas seam-side down in the baking dish.

Pour the remaining enchilada sauce over the top of the enchiladas.

Sprinkle the shredded cheddar cheese over the top of the enchiladas.

Bake in the preheated oven for 20-25 minutes, or until the cheese is melted and bubbly.

Garnish with fresh cilantro and serve hot.

51. Black Bean and Corn Enchiladas

Ingredients:

- 1 onion, chopped
- 2 garlic cloves, minced
- 1 can (15 oz) black beans, drained and rinsed
- 1 can (15 oz) corn, drained
- 1 tsp ground cumin
- Salt and pepper, to taste
- 8-10 corn tortillas
- 1 1/2 cups shredded cheddar cheese
- 1 can (15 oz) enchilada sauce

Instructions:

Preheat the oven to 350°F.

In a large skillet, sauté the chopped onion and garlic until fragrant, about 2-3 minutes.

Add the black beans, corn, cumin, salt, and pepper to the skillet and stir until well combined.

Warm the corn tortillas in the microwave or on a griddle until they are soft and pliable.

Pour a small amount of enchilada sauce in the bottom of a 9x13 inch baking dish.

Place a generous spoonful of the black bean and corn mixture onto each tortilla and roll up tightly.

Place the rolled up tortillas seam-side down in the baking dish.

Pour the remaining enchilada sauce over the top of the enchiladas.

Sprinkle the shredded cheddar cheese over the top of the enchiladas.

Bake in the preheated oven for 20-25 minutes, or until the cheese is melted and bubbly.

Garnish with fresh cilantro and serve hot.

52. Butternut Squash and Spinach Enchiladas

Ingredients:

1 butternut squash, peeled and chopped
1 onion, chopped
2 garlic cloves, minced
1 can (15 oz) black beans, drained and rinsed
1 cup chopped spinach
1 tsp ground cumin
Salt and pepper, to taste
8-10 corn tortillas
1 1/2 cups shredded Monterey Jack cheese
1 can (15 oz) enchilada sauce

Instructions:

Preheat the oven to 350°F.
In a large skillet, sauté the chopped onion and garlic until fragrant, about 2-3 minutes.
Add the chopped butternut squash to the skillet and cook until tender, about 10-12 minutes.
Add the black beans, spinach, cumin, salt, and pepper to the skillet and stir until well combined.
Warm the corn tortillas in the microwave or on a griddle until they are soft and pliable.
Pour a small amount of enchilada sauce in the bottom of a 9x13 inch baking dish.
Place a generous spoonful of the butternut squash and spinach mixture onto each tortilla and roll up tightly.
Place the rolled up tortillas seam-side down in the baking dish.
Pour the remaining enchilada sauce over the top of the enchiladas.
Sprinkle the shredded Monterey Jack cheese over the top of the enchiladas.
Bake in the preheated oven for 20-25 minutes, or until the cheese is melted and bubbly.
Garnish with fresh cilantro and serve hot.

53. Zucchini and Corn Enchiladas

Ingredients:

1 onion, chopped
2 garlic cloves, minced
2 zucchini, chopped
1 can (15 oz) corn, drained
1 tsp ground cumin
Salt and pepper, to taste
8-10 corn tortillas
1 1/2 cups shredded cheddar cheese
1 can (15 oz) enchilada sauce

Instructions:
Preheat the oven to 350°F.
In a large skillet, sauté the chopped onion and garlic until fragrant, about 2-3 minutes.
Add the chopped zucchini and corn to the skillet and cook until tender, about 10-12 minutes.
Add the cumin, salt, and pepper to the skillet and stir until well combined.
5. Warm the corn tortillas in the microwave or on a griddle until they are soft and pliable.
Pour a small amount of enchilada sauce in the bottom of a 9x13 inch baking dish.
Place a generous spoonful of the zucchini and corn mixture onto each tortilla and roll up tightly.
Place the rolled up tortillas seam-side down in the baking dish.
Pour the remaining enchilada sauce over the top of the enchiladas.
Sprinkle the shredded cheddar cheese over the top of the enchiladas.
Bake in the preheated oven for 20-25 minutes, or until the cheese is melted and bubbly.
Garnish with fresh cilantro and serve hot.

54. Portobello Mushroom Enchiladas

Ingredients:
- 2 tbsp olive oil
- 4 portobello mushrooms, sliced
- 1 onion, chopped
- 2 garlic cloves, minced
- 1 can (15 oz) black beans, drained and rinsed
- 1 tsp ground cumin
- Salt and pepper, to taste
- 8-10 corn tortillas
- 1 1/2 cups shredded Monterey Jack cheese
- 1 can (15 oz) enchilada sauce

Instructions:

Preheat the oven to 350°F.

In a large skillet, heat the olive oil over medium-high heat.

Add the sliced portobello mushrooms to the skillet and sauté until tender and browned, about 5-7 minutes.

Add the chopped onion and garlic to the skillet and sauté until fragrant, about 2-3 minutes.

Add the black beans, cumin, salt, and pepper to the skillet and stir until well combined.

Warm the corn tortillas in the microwave or on a griddle until they are soft and pliable

Gilbert A

continue

Pour a small amount of enchilada sauce in the bottom of a 9x13 inch baking dish.

Place a generous spoonful of the mushroom and black bean mixture onto each tortilla and roll up tightly.

Place the rolled up tortillas seam-side down in the baking dish.

Pour the remaining enchilada sauce over the top of the enchiladas.

Sprinkle the shredded Monterey Jack cheese over the top of the enchiladas.

Bake in the preheated oven for 20-25 minutes, or until the cheese is melted and bubbly.

Garnish with fresh cilantro and serve hot.

VEGAN ENCHILADAS

55. Vegan Black Bean and Corn Enchiladas

Ingredients:
- 1 can (15 oz) black beans, drained and rinsed
- 1 can (15 oz) corn, drained
- 1/2 cup salsa
- 1/2 cup diced onion
- 1/2 cup chopped fresh cilantro
- 1 tsp cumin
- 1 tsp chili powder
- 8-10 corn tortillas
- 1 cup vegan shredded cheddar cheese
- Salt and pepper, to taste

Instructions:
Preheat oven to 350°F.
In a large bowl, mix together the black beans, corn, salsa, onion, cilantro, cumin, and chili powder.
Season with salt and pepper to taste.
Spread a small amount of the bean mixture onto each tortilla and roll up tightly.
Place the rolled-up tortillas seam-side down in a 9x13 inch baking dish.
Sprinkle with vegan shredded cheese and bake for 20-25 minutes, until cheese is melted and bubbly.

56. Vegan Chickpea Enchiladas

Ingredients:
- 2 cans (15 oz each) chickpeas, drained and rinsed
- 1 onion, chopped
- 2 cloves garlic, minced
- 1 can (10 oz) red enchilada sauce
- 8-10 corn tortillas
- 1 cup vegan shredded cheddar cheese
- Salt and pepper, to taste

Instructions:
Preheat oven to 350°F.
In a large skillet, cook the onion and garlic over medium heat until tender.
Add the chickpeas to the skillet and stir to combine.
Stir in the red enchilada sauce, and season with salt and pepper to taste.
Spread a small amount of the chickpea mixture onto each tortilla and roll up tightly.
Place the rolled-up tortillas seam-side down in a 9x13 inch baking dish.
Sprinkle with vegan shredded cheese and bake for 20-25 minutes, until cheese is melted and bubbly.

57. Vegan Sweet Potato Enchiladas

Ingredients:
- 2 large sweet potatoes, peeled and diced
- 1 can (15 oz) black beans, drained and rinsed
- 1 onion, chopped
- 2 cloves garlic, minced
- 1 can (10 oz) green enchilada sauce
- 8-10 corn tortillas
- 1 cup vegan shredded cheddar cheese
- Salt and pepper, to taste

Instructions:
1. Preheat oven to 350°F.
2. Steam the diced sweet potatoes until tender.
3. In a large skillet, cook the onion and garlic over medium heat until tender.
4. Add the black beans and steamed sweet potatoes to the skillet and stir to combine.
5. Stir in the green enchilada sauce, and season with salt and pepper to taste.
6. Spread a small amount of the sweet potato mixture onto each tortilla and roll up tightly.
7. Place the rolled-up tortillas seam-side down in a 9x13 inch baking dish.
8. Sprinkle with vegan shredded cheese and bake for 20-25 minutes, until cheese is melted and bubbly.

58. Vegan Spinach and Tofu Enchiladas

Ingredients:
- 1 block (14 oz) firm tofu, drained and crumbled
- 2 cups fresh spinach, chopped
- 1 onion, chopped
- 2 cloves garlic, minced
- 1 can (10 oz) red enchilada sauce
- 8-10 corn tortillas
- 1 cup vegan shredded cheddar cheese
- Salt and pepper, to taste

Instructions:
Preheat oven to 350°F.
In a large skillet, cook the onion and garlic over medium heat until tender.
Add the crumbled tofu and chopped spinach to the skillet and stir to combine.
Stir in the red enchilada sauce, and season with salt and pepper to taste.
Spread a small amount of the tofu and spinach mixture onto each tortilla and roll up tightly.
Place the rolled-up tortillas seam-side down in a 9x13 inch baking dish.
Sprinkle with vegan shredded cheese and bake for 20-25 minutes, until cheese is melted and bubbly.

59. Vegan Jackfruit Enchiladas

Ingredients:
- 2 cans (20 oz total) jackfruit, drained and shredded
- 1 onion, chopped
- 2 cloves garlic, minced
- 1 can (10 oz) green enchilada sauce
- 8-10 corn tortillas
- 1 cup vegan shredded cheddar cheese
- Salt and pepper, to taste

Instructions:
Preheat oven to 350°F.
In a large skillet, cook the onion and garlic over medium heat until tender.
Add the shredded jackfruit to the skillet and stir to combine.
Stir in the green enchilada sauce, and season with salt and pepper to taste.
Spread a small amount of the jackfruit mixture onto each tortilla and roll up tightly.
Place the rolled-up tortillas seam-side down in a 9x13 inch baking dish.
Sprinkle with vegan shredded cheese and bake for 20-25 minutes, until cheese is melted and bubbly.

60. Vegan Lentil Enchiladas

Ingredients:
1 cup dry lentils, rinsed and drained
1 onion, chopped
2 cloves garlic, minced
1 can (10 oz) red enchilada sauce
8-10 corn tortillas
1 cup vegan shredded cheddar cheese
Salt and pepper, to taste

Instructions:
Preheat oven to 350°F.
In a large pot, cook the lentils according to package instructions until tender.
In a large skillet, cook the onion and garlic over medium heat until tender.
Add the cooked lentils to the skillet and stir to combine.
Stir in the red enchilada sauce, and season with salt and pepper to taste.
Spread a small amount of the lentil mixture onto each tortilla and roll up tightly.
Place the rolled-up tortillas seam-side down in a 9x13 inch baking dish.
Sprinkle with vegan shredded cheese and bake for 20-25 minutes, until cheese is melted and bubbly.

61. Vegan Tempeh Enchiladas

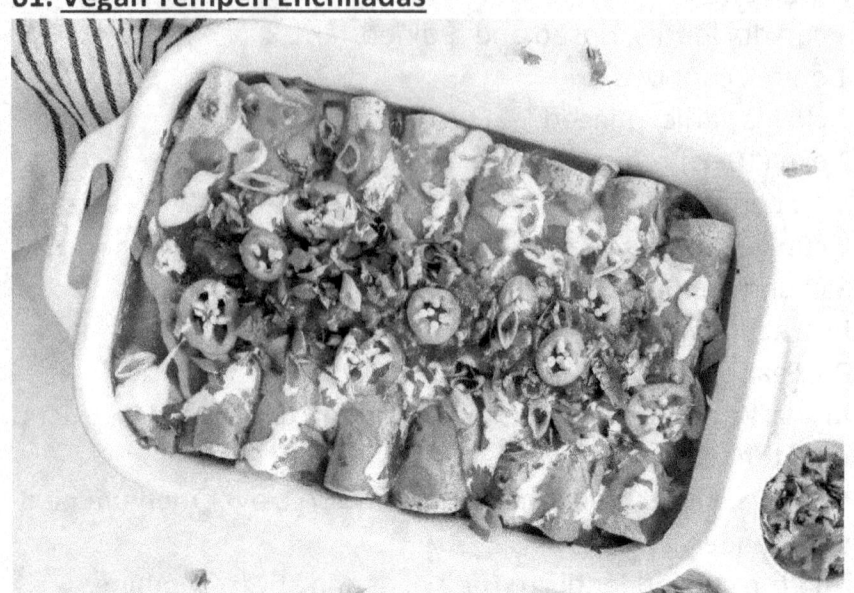

Ingredients:
- 1 package (8 oz) tempeh, crumbled
- 1 onion, chopped
- 2 cloves garlic, minced
- 1 can (10 oz) red enchilada sauce
- 8-10 corn tortillas
- 1 cup vegan shredded cheddar cheese
- Salt and pepper, to taste

Instructions:

Preheat oven to 350°F.

In a large skillet, cook the onion and garlic over medium heat until tender.

Add the crumbled tempeh to the skillet and stir to combine.

Stir in the red enchilada sauce, and season with salt and pepper to taste.

Spread a small amount of the tempeh mixture onto each tortilla and roll up tightly.

Place the rolled-up tortillas seam-side down in a 9x13 inch baking dish.

Sprinkle with vegan shredded cheese and bake for 20-25 minutes, until cheese is melted and bubbly.

62. Vegan Sweet Potato Enchiladas

Ingredients:
2 sweet potatoes, peeled and diced
1 onion, chopped
2 cloves garlic, minced
1 can (10 oz) green enchilada sauce
8-10 corn tortillas
1 cup vegan shredded cheddar cheese
Salt and pepper, to taste

Instructions:
Preheat oven to 350°F.
In a large skillet, cook the onion and garlic over medium heat until tender.
Add the diced sweet potatoes to the skillet and cook until tender, stirring occasionally.
Stir in the green enchilada sauce, and season with salt and pepper to taste.
Spread a small amount of the sweet potato mixture onto each tortilla and roll up tightly.
Place the rolled-up tortillas seam-side down in a 9x13 inch baking dish.
Sprinkle with vegan shredded cheese and bake for 20-25 minutes, until cheese is melted and bubbly.

63. Vegan Quinoa Enchiladas

Ingredients:
1 cup quinoa, rinsed and drained
1 onion, chopped
2 cloves garlic, minced
1 can (10 oz) red enchilada sauce
8-10 corn tortillas
1 cup vegan shredded cheddar cheese
Salt and pepper, to taste

Instructions:
Preheat oven to 350°F.
In a large pot, cook the quinoa according to package instructions.
In a large skillet, cook the onion and garlic over medium heat until tender.
Add the cooked quinoa to the skillet and stir to combine.
Stir in the red enchilada sauce, and season with salt and pepper to taste.
Spread a small amount of the quinoa mixture onto each tortilla and roll up tightly.
Place the rolled-up tortillas seam-side down in a 9x13 inch baking dish.
Sprinkle with vegan shredded cheese and bake for 20-25 minutes, until cheese is melted and bubbly.

FRUIT ENCHILADAS

64. Strawberry Cream Cheese Enchiladas

Ingredients:
- 10 flour tortillas
- 1 package (8 oz) cream cheese, softened
- 1/4 cup granulated sugar
- 2 cups fresh strawberries, sliced
- 1/4 cup unsalted butter, melted
- 1/2 cup granulated sugar
- 1/2 tsp ground cinnamon
- Whipped cream, for serving

Instructions:
Preheat the oven to 350°F.
In a medium bowl, beat together the cream cheese and 1/4 cup sugar until smooth.
Lay a tortilla on a flat surface and spread about 1 1/2 tablespoons of the cream cheese mixture in the center.
Arrange a few slices of strawberries on top of the cream cheese mixture.
Roll up the tortilla tightly and place it seam-side down in a 9x13 inch baking dish.
Repeat with the remaining tortillas, cream cheese mixture, and strawberries.
In a small bowl, mix together the melted butter, 1/2 cup sugar, and cinnamon.
Pour the butter mixture over the enchiladas.
Bake for 20-25 minutes, or until the enchiladas are golden brown and crispy. Serve with whipped cream.

65. Pineapple Enchiladas

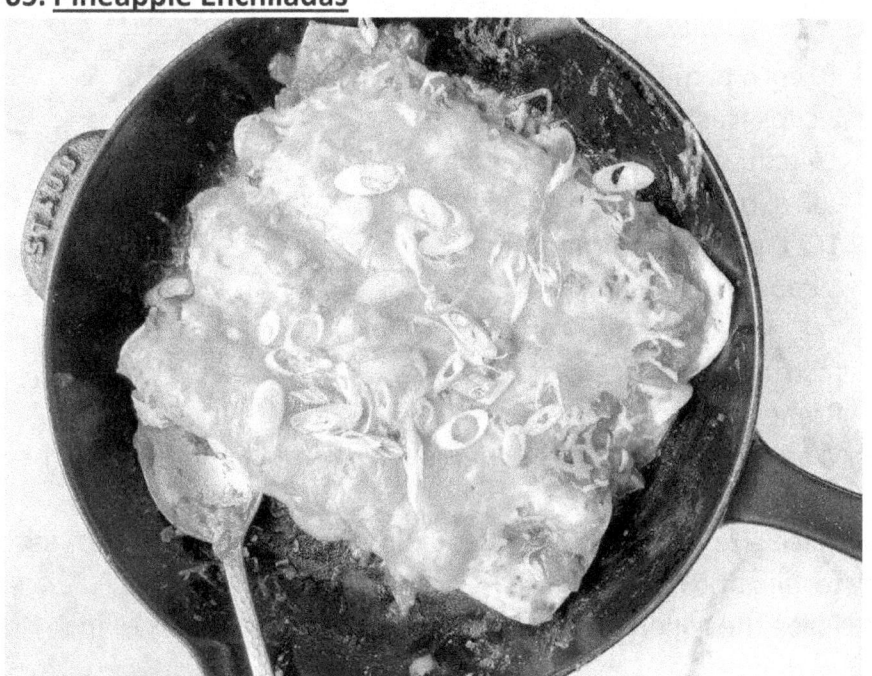

Ingredients:

- 10 corn tortillas
- 2 cups fresh pineapple, diced
- 1/4 cup unsalted butter, melted
- 1/2 cup granulated sugar
- 1/2 tsp ground cinnamon
- 1 cup heavy cream
- 1/2 cup sweetened condensed milk

Instructions:

Preheat the oven to 350°F.

Warm the tortillas in the microwave or on a griddle until they are soft and pliable.

Place a few spoonfuls of diced pineapple in the center of each tortilla and roll up tightly.

Place the rolled up tortillas seam-side down in a 9x13 inch baking dish.

In a small bowl, mix together the melted butter, 1/2 cup sugar, and cinnamon.

Pour the butter mixture over the top of the enchiladas.

Bake for 20-25 minutes, or until the enchiladas are golden brown and crispy.

In a medium bowl, whisk together the heavy cream and sweetened condensed milk until soft peaks form.

Serve the enchiladas hot with a dollop of whipped cream on top.

66. Apple Enchiladas

Ingredients:

10 flour tortillas
2 cups peeled and diced apples
1/2 cup unsalted butter, melted
1/2 cup granulated sugar
1 tsp ground cinnamon
1/2 cup chopped walnuts (optional)
Vanilla ice cream, for serving

Instructions:

Preheat the oven to 350°F.
In a medium bowl, mix together the diced apples, 1/4 cup melted butter, 1/4 cup sugar, and cinnamon.
Warm the tortillas in the microwave or on a griddle until they are soft and pliable.
Spoon some of the apple mixture onto each tortilla and roll up tightly.
Place the rolled up tortillas seam-side down in a 9x13 inch baking dish.
In a small bowl, mix together the remaining melted butter, sugar, and chopped walnuts (if using).
Pour the butter mixture over the top of the enchiladas.
Bake for 20-25 minutes, or until the enchiladas are golden brown and crispy.
Serve the enchiladas hot with a scoop of vanilla ice cream on top.

67. Mixed Berry Enchiladas

Ingredients:

10 flour tortillas
2 cups mixed fresh berries (such as strawberries, blueberries, and raspberries), chopped
1/4 cup unsalted butter, melted
1/2 cup granulated sugar
1/2 tsp ground cinnamon
Whipped cream, for serving

Instructions:

Preheat the oven to 350°F.
In a medium bowl, mix together the chopped berries, 1/4 cup sugar, and cinnamon.
Warm the tortillas in the microwave or on a griddle until they are soft and pliable.
Spoon some of the berry mixture onto each tortilla and roll up tightly.
Place the rolled up tortillas seam-side down in a 9x13 inch baking dish.
In a small bowl, mix together the melted butter and remaining sugar.
Pour the butter mixture over the top of the enchiladas.
Bake for 20-25 minutes, or until the enchiladas are golden brown and crispy.
Serve the enchiladas hot with whipped cream.

68. Peach Enchiladas

Ingredients:

10 flour tortillas
2 cups peeled and diced peaches
1/2 cup unsalted butter, melted
1/2 cup granulated sugar
1 tsp ground cinnamon
Vanilla ice cream, for serving

Instructions:

Preheat the oven to 350°F.
In a medium bowl, mix together the diced peaches, 1/4 cup melted butter, 1/4 cup sugar, and cinnamon.
Warm the tortillas in the microwave or on a griddle until they are soft and pliable.
Spoon some of the peach mixture onto each tortilla and roll up tightly.
Place the rolled up tortillas seam-side down in a 9x13 inch baking dish.
In a small bowl, mix together the remaining melted butter and sugar.
Pour the butter mixture over the top of the enchiladas.
Bake for 20-25 minutes, or until the enchiladas are golden brown and crispy.
Serve the enchiladas hot with a scoop of vanilla ice cream on top.

LEGUMES AND GRAINS

69. Quinoa Enchilada Casserole

Makes: 6

INGREDIENTS:
- 1 1/2 cups uncooked quinoa
- 1 cup enchilada sauce
- 2 1/4 cups vegetable broth
- 1 medium onion, chopped
- 14.5oz diced tomatoes, undrained
- 15oz corn kernels, drained and rinsed
- 15oz can black beans, drained and rinsed
- 1 tablespoon chili powder
- 1 1/2 teaspoons cumin powder
- 1/2 teaspoon ground black pepper
- 3/4 cup green bell pepper, chopped
- 3/4 cup red bell pepper, chopped
- 5 cloves garlic, minced
- 1 1/4 cups plant-based mozzarella cheese shreds
- 1 1/2 tablespoons lime juice
- 1/2 teaspoon sea salt
- Chopped parsley, chopped tomatoes, plant-based sour cream

INSTRUCTIONS:
a) Using the slow cooker, combine all ingredients except the cheese and the lime with the vegetable broth. Stir a few times to combine thoroughly.
b) Set the slow cooker setting to high for 2 to 2½ hours.
c) Open the slow cooker and add the lime juice and 12 slices of cheese.
d) Stir the mixture, then smooth it back out flat. Sprinkle the remaining cheese on top, then replace the lid and cook for 10 minutes.
e) Serve with your favorite toppings - avocado, chopped green onions, parsley, sour cream, and tomato.

70. Sweet Potato and Black Bean Enchiladas

2 medium sweet potatoes, peeled and diced
1 can of black beans, drained and rinsed
1 diced onion
2 cloves of garlic
1 can of green enchilada sauce
12 corn tortillas
Salt and pepper to taste

Preheat the oven to 375°F. In a skillet, cook the onion and garlic until softened. Add the sweet potatoes and black beans, and season with salt and pepper. In a saucepan, heat the enchilada sauce over medium heat. Dip the tortillas in the sauce and place them in a 9x13 inch baking dish. Fill each tortilla with the sweet potato and black bean mixture and roll it up. Pour the remaining sauce over the enchiladas and bake for 25-30 minutes.

71. Black Bean Enchiladas

Ingredients:
1 can (15 oz) black beans, drained and rinsed
1 onion, chopped
2 cloves garlic, minced
1 can (10 oz) enchilada sauce
8-10 corn tortillas
1 cup shredded cheddar cheese
Salt and pepper, to taste

Instructions:
Preheat oven to 350°F.
In a large skillet, cook the onion and garlic over medium heat until tender.
Add the black beans to the skillet and stir to combine.
Stir in the enchilada sauce, and season with salt and pepper to taste.
Spread a small amount of the black bean mixture onto each tortilla and roll up tightly.
Place the rolled-up tortillas seam-side down in a 9x13 inch baking dish.
Pour the remaining black bean mixture over the tortillas, and sprinkle with shredded cheese.
Bake for 20-25 minutes, until cheese is melted and bubbly

72. <u>Mixed Bean Enchiladas</u>

Ingredients:

10 corn tortillas
1 can (15 oz) black beans, drained and rinsed
1 can (15 oz) kidney beans, drained and rinsed
1 can (15 oz) pinto beans, drained and rinsed
1 can (4 oz) diced green chilies
1/2 cup chopped onion
1/2 cup chopped green bell pepper
2 cloves garlic, minced
1 tsp ground cumin
1 tsp chili powder
2 cups enchilada sauce
1 cup shredded cheddar cheese
1/4 cup chopped fresh cilantro

Instructions:

Preheat the oven to 375°F.
In a large bowl, mix together the black beans, kidney beans, pinto beans, green chilies, onion, bell pepper, garlic, cumin, and chili powder.
Warm the tortillas in the microwave or on a griddle until they are soft and pliable.
Spoon some of the bean mixture onto each tortilla and roll up tightly.
Place the rolled up tortillas seam-side down in a 9x13 inch baking dish.
Pour the enchilada sauce over the top of the enchiladas.
Sprinkle the shredded cheese over the top of the enchiladas.
Bake for 20-25 minutes, or until the enchiladas are golden brown and the cheese is melted.
Sprinkle the chopped cilantro over the top of the enchiladas before serving.

SAUCES

73. Easy Red Enchilada Sauce

Makes: 7

INGREDIENTS:
- Onion and Garlic
- 1 cup white onion, chopped
- 4 cloves garlic, peeled and smashed
- 3 tablespoons vegetable broth
- Peppers
- 2 dried Arbol chilies, stems removed
- 7 mild dried chilies
- 1 cup water
- 2 cups vegetable broth
- Spices
- 1/4 cup tomato paste
- 1 teaspoon ground smoked paprika
- 1 teaspoon ground cumin
- 1 teaspoon dried oregano
- 1/2 teaspoon sea salt

INSTRUCTIONS:
a) In a rimmed skillet over medium heat, add vegetable broth.
b) Sauté the onion and garlic for 4-5 minutes. Cook until lightly browned and tender.
c) Cook for 2 minutes with the dried chilies. Then pour in the vegetable broth and water.
d) Bring the water to a boil, then reduce the heat and cover. Allow for a 15-minute simmer.
e) Combine tomato paste, cumin, paprika, salt, and oregano in a mixing bowl (optional). Cook for at least 5 minutes, stirring occasionally or until the peppers are tender.
f) Blend until creamy and smooth in a high-speed blender. Taste and adjust the flavor as desired. Serve right away.

74. Red Enchilada Sauce

2 tablespoons vegetable oil
2 tablespoons all-purpose flour
4 tablespoons chili powder
1/2 teaspoon garlic powder
1/2 teaspoon onion powder
1/2 teaspoon ground cumin
2 cups chicken or vegetable broth
Salt to taste

Heat oil in a saucepan over medium heat. Add flour and stir for 1 minute. Add chili powder, garlic powder, onion powder, and cumin. Stir until combined. Gradually add broth while whisking constantly. Bring to a boil and reduce heat to low. Simmer for 10-15 minutes, stirring occasionally. Season with salt to taste.

75. Green Enchilada Sauce

1 pound tomatillos, husked and rinsed
2 jalapenos, seeded and chopped
1 onion, chopped
3 cloves garlic, minced
1/2 cup fresh cilantro, chopped
1 tablespoon lime juice
Salt to taste

Place tomatillos, jalapenos, onion, and garlic in a blender or food processor. Blend until smooth. Transfer to a saucepan and bring to a simmer over medium heat. Cook for 10-15 minutes, stirring occasionally. Stir in cilantro and lime juice. Season with salt to taste.

76. Ancho Chili Enchilada Sauce

2 ancho chili peppers, stemmed and seeded
1 onion, chopped
3 cloves garlic, minced
1 teaspoon cumin
1 teaspoon dried oregano
1 tablespoon vegetable oil
2 cups chicken or vegetable broth
Salt to taste

Toast ancho chili peppers in a dry skillet over medium heat until fragrant, about 1 minute. Add onion, garlic, cumin, and oregano. Cook until onion is soft, about 5 minutes. Transfer mixture to a blender or food processor. Add broth and blend until smooth. Heat oil in a saucepan over medium heat. Add the chili pepper mixture and bring to a simmer. Cook for 10-15 minutes, stirring occasionally. Season with salt to taste.

77. Roasted Tomato Enchilada Sauce

- 6 roma tomatoes, halved
- 1 onion, chopped
- 3 cloves garlic, minced
- 2 tablespoons vegetable oil
- 2 teaspoons chili powder
- 1/2 teaspoon cumin
- 2 cups chicken or vegetable broth
- Salt to taste

Preheat oven to 400°F. Arrange tomatoes on a baking sheet, cut side up. Roast for 20-25 minutes, until tomatoes are tender and lightly browned. Heat oil in a saucepan over medium heat. Add onion and garlic, and cook until onion is soft, about 5 minutes. Add chili powder and cumin, and cook for 1 minute. Add roasted tomatoes and broth. Bring to a boil, reduce heat to low, and simmer for 10-15 minutes. Season with salt to taste.

78. Chipotle Enchilada Sauce

2 tablespoons vegetable oil
2 tablespoons all-purpose flour
2 tablespoons chipotle chili powder
1/2 teaspoon garlic powder
1/2 teaspoon onion powder
1/2 teaspoon cumin
2 cups chicken or vegetable broth
Salt to taste

Heat oil in a saucepan over medium heat. Add flour and stir for 1 minute. Add chipotle chili powder, garlic powder, onion powder, and cumin. Stir until combined. Gradually add broth while whisking constantly. Bring to a boil and reduce heat to low. Simmer for 10-15 minutes, stirring occasionally. Season with salt to taste.

79. Creamy Enchilada Sauce

2 tablespoons butter
2 tablespoons all-purpose flour
2 cups chicken or vegetable broth
1 cup heavy cream
1 teaspoon chili powder
1/2 teaspoon cumin
Salt to taste

Melt butter in a saucepan over medium heat. Add flour and stir for 1 minute. Gradually add broth while whisking constantly. Bring to a boil and reduce heat to low. Simmer for 10-15 minutes, stirring occasionally. Stir in heavy cream, chili powder, and cumin. Cook for 5 minutes, stirring constantly. Season with salt to taste.

80. Smoky Enchilada Sauce

- 1 tablespoon vegetable oil
- 1 onion, chopped
- 2 cloves garlic, minced
- 2 tablespoons chili powder
- 1 teaspoon smoked paprika
- 1/2 teaspoon cumin
- 2 cups chicken or vegetable broth
- Salt to taste

Heat oil in a saucepan over medium heat. Add onion and garlic, and cook until onion is soft, about 5 minutes. Add chili powder, smoked paprika, and cumin. Cook for 1 minute. Gradually add broth while whisking constantly. Bring to a boil and reduce heat to low. Simmer for 10-15 minutes, stirring occasionally. Season with salt to taste.

81. Mole Enchilada Sauce

1/2 cup vegetable oil
2 ancho chili peppers, stemmed and seeded
2 pasilla chili peppers, stemmed and seeded
1 onion, chopped
3 cloves garlic, minced
2 tablespoons cocoa powder
1 teaspoon cinnamon
1/2 teaspoon cumin
2 cups chicken or vegetable broth
Salt to taste

Heat oil in a skillet over medium heat. Add chili peppers and cook until slightly charred, about 1 minute per side. Remove peppers from skillet and let cool. Add onion and garlic to skillet, and cook until onion is soft, about 5 minutes. Transfer mixture to a blender or food processor. Add cocoa powder, cinnamon, and cumin. Add the cooled peppers and 1 cup of broth. Blend until smooth. Heat the remaining broth in a saucepan over medium heat. Add the blended mixture and simmer for 10-15 minutes, stirring occasionally. Season with salt to taste.

82. Ranchero Enchilada Sauce

1 tablespoon vegetable oil
1 onion, chopped
2 cloves garlic, minced
2 teaspoons chili powder
1/2 teaspoon cumin
1 can (14 ounces) diced tomatoes
1 can (8 ounces) tomato sauce
Salt to taste

Heat oil in a saucepan over medium heat. Add onion and garlic, and cook until onion is soft, about 5 minutes. Add chili powder and cumin. Cook for 1 minute. Add diced tomatoes and tomato sauce. Bring to a boil, reduce heat to low, and simmer for 10-15 minutes, stirring occasionally. Season with salt to taste.

83. White Enchilada Sauce

2 tablespoons butter
2 tablespoons all-purpose flour
2 cups chicken or vegetable broth
1 cup sour cream
1 can (4 ounces) chopped green chilies
Salt to taste

Melt butter in a saucepan over medium heat. Add flour and stir for 1 minute. Gradually add broth while whisking constantly. Bring to a boil and reduce heat to low. Simmer for 10-15 minutes, stirring occasionally. Stir in sour cream and green chilies. Cook for 5 minutes, stirring constantly. Season with salt to taste.

84. Whiskey Chipotle Enchilada Sauce

2 tablespoons vegetable oil
1 onion, chopped
3 cloves garlic, minced
2 tablespoons adobo sauce
1 teaspoon chili powder
1/2 teaspoon cumin
2 cups chicken or vegetable broth
Salt to taste
2 tablespoons whiskey

Heat oil in a saucepan over medium heat. Add onion and garlic, and cook until onion is soft, about 5 minutes. Add adobo sauce, whiskey, chili powder, and cumin. Cook for 1 minute. Gradually add broth while whisking constantly. Bring to a boil and reduce heat to low. Simmer for 10-15 minutes, stirring occasionally. Season with salt to taste.

85. Vegan Cashew Cheese Sauce

Makes: 6 Servings

INGREDIENTS:
- 1.5 cups Cashews soaked & soaked overnight
- ¾ cup water
- ½ cup Nutritional Yeast
- 1 tablespoon Mustard or Dijon Mustard
- 3 tablespoon Lemon Juice
- 1 teaspoon smoked paprika
- ½ tablespoon Turmeric
- 1 tablespoon Garlic Powder
- 1 teaspoon Salt
- 3 cloves garlic, peeled

INSTRUCTIONS
a) Drain cashews then add all ingredients into a blender.
b) Blend on high until creamy and smooth.

86. Fresh Tomato Salsa

Makes: 2 cups

INGREDIENTS:
- 5 ripe Roma or plum tomatoes, chopped
- 1 serrano chile, seeded and minced
- ¼ cup chopped red onion
- 1 garlic clove, minced
- 1 tablespoon minced fresh cilantro
- 1 tablespoon fresh lime juice
- ½ teaspoon salt

INSTRUCTIONS

a) In a glass bowl, combine all the ingredients and mix well.

b) Cover and set aside for 30 minutes before serving. If not using right away, cover and refrigerate until ready to use.

c) This salsa tastes best if used on the same day it is made, but properly stored, it will keep for up to 2 days.

87. Spicy Mango And Red Pepper Salsa

Makes: 2½ cups

INGREDIENTS:
- 1 ripe mango, peeled, pitted, and cut into ¼-inch dice
- 1/3 cup minced red onion
- 1 small red bell pepper, chopped
- 1 small jalapeño, seeded and minced
- 2 tablespoons chopped fresh parsley or cilantro
- 1 tablespoon fresh lime juice
- Salt

INSTRUCTIONS
a) In a glass bowl, combine all the ingredients, mix well, cover, and set aside for 30 minutes before serving. If not using right away, refrigerate until ready to use.
b) This salsa tastes best if used on the same day it is made, but properly stored, it will keep for up to 2 days.

88. Chipotle-Tomato Salsa

Makes: 2 cups

INGREDIENTS:
- 2 ripe tomatoes, chopped
- 1/3 cup minced red onion
- 1 canned chipotle in adobo
- ¼ cup chopped fresh cilantro
- 2 tablespoons fresh lime juice
- ¼ teaspoon salt

INSTRUCTIONS
a) In a glass bowl, combine all the ingredients.
b) Refrigerating until ready to use.
c) Properly stored, it will keep for up to 2 days.

89. Pineapple-Papaya Salsa

Makes: 3 cups

INGREDIENTS:
- 2 cups chopped fresh pineapple
- 1 ripe papaya, peeled, seeded, and cut into ¼-inch dice
- ½ cup minced red onion
- ¼ cup chopped fresh cilantro or parsley
- 2 tablespoons fresh lime juice
- 1 teaspoon cider vinegar
- 2 teaspoons sugar
- ¼ teaspoon salt
- 1 small hot red chile, seeded and minced

INSTRUCTIONS

a) In a glass bowl, combine all the ingredients, mix well, cover, and set aside at room temperature for 30 minutes before serving or refrigerating until ready to use.

b) This salsa tastes best if used on the same day it is made, but properly stored, it will keep for up to 2 days.

90. Tomatillo Salsa

Makes: 1½ cups

INGREDIENTS:
- 5 tomatillos, husked and chopped
- 1/3 cup chopped sweet yellow onion
- 1/3 cup chopped fresh cilantro
- 1 small jalapeño, seeded and minced
- 1 tablespoon fresh lime juice
- 1 tablespoon whole capers, plus 1 teaspoon minced
- ½ teaspoon salt

INSTRUCTIONS
a) In a glass bowl, combine all the ingredients, and mix well.
b) Set aside for 30 minutes before serving.
c) Properly stored, it will keep in the refrigerator for up to 2 days.

91. Salsa Verde

Makes: 1¼ cups

INGREDIENTS:
- 4 or 5 tomatillos, husked and coarsely chopped
- 1 medium shallot, coarsely chopped
- 1 garlic clove, chopped
- 1 serrano chile, seeded and chopped
- 1¼ cup fresh cilantro leaves
- 1 tablespoon fresh lime juice
- Pinch sugar
- ½ teaspoon salt
- 1/8 teaspoon freshly ground black pepper

INSTRUCTIONS

a) In a food processor, combine the tomatillos, shallot, garlic, chile (if using), parsley, and cilantro and pulse until finely chopped.

b) Add the remaining ingredients and pulse until well mixed, but still coarsely textured.

c) Transfer to a glass bowl, cover, and set aside at room temperature for 30 minutes before serving or refrigerate until ready to use.

d) Properly stored, it will keep for up to 2 days.

92. Roasted Red Salsa

Makes: 2 cups

INGREDIENTS:
- 15 ounces diced fire-roasted tomatoes, drained
- 1 clove garlic, roughly chopped
- ½ cup white onion, roughly chopped
- ¼ cup fresh cilantro leaves
- ½ medium jalapeño, roughly chopped
- 1 tablespoon lime juice
- ½ teaspoon fine sea salt

INSTRUCTIONS:
a) In a food processor, pulse the garlic to chop it more finely.
b) Add the tomatoes and all of the remaining juice from the can.
c) Add the onion, cilantro, jalapeño, lime juice, and salt.
d) Process the mixture until it is mostly smooth and no big chunks of tomato or onion remain, scraping down the sides as necessary.
e) Serve the salsa immediately or store it for later.

93. Tomatillo Enchilada Sauce

1 tablespoon vegetable oil
1 onion, chopped
3 cloves garlic, minced
1 pound tomatillos, husked and chopped
1 jalapeño pepper, seeded and chopped
2 cups chicken or vegetable broth
1/4 cup chopped cilantro
Salt to taste

Heat oil in a saucepan over medium heat. Add onion and garlic, and cook until onion is soft, about 5 minutes. Add tomatillos and jalapeño. Cook for 5 minutes. Gradually add broth while whisking constantly. Bring to a boil and reduce heat to low. Simmer for 10-15 minutes, stirring occasionally. Add cilantro and puree in a blender or food processor. Season with salt to taste.

94. Pasilla Enchilada Sauce

2 pasilla chili peppers, stemmed and seeded
1 onion, chopped
3 cloves garlic, minced
1 tablespoon vegetable oil
1 teaspoon oregano
2 cups chicken or vegetable broth
Salt to taste

Toast pasilla peppers in a dry skillet over medium heat until slightly charred, about 1 minute per side. Remove from skillet and let cool. Add peppers to a blender or food processor and puree. Heat oil in a saucepan over medium heat. Add onion and garlic, and cook until onion is soft, about 5 minutes. Add oregano and cook for 1 minute. Gradually add broth while whisking constantly. Bring to a boil and reduce heat to low. Simmer for 10-15 minutes, stirring occasionally. Add pureed pasilla peppers and season with salt to taste.

95. Three Pepper Enchilada Sauce

1 red bell pepper, chopped
1 green bell pepper, chopped
1 jalapeño pepper, seeded and chopped
1 onion, chopped
3 cloves garlic, minced
1 teaspoon chili powder
1/2 teaspoon cumin
2 cups chicken or vegetable broth
Salt to taste

Heat oil in a saucepan over medium heat. Add bell peppers, jalapeño, onion, and garlic, and cook until vegetables are soft, about 5 minutes. Add chili powder and cumin. Cook for 1 minute. Gradually add broth while whisking constantly. Bring to a boil and reduce heat to low. Simmer for 10-15 minutes, stirring occasionally. Puree in a blender or food processor. Season with salt to taste.

96. Ancho Enchilada Sauce

2 dried ancho chili peppers, stemmed and seeded
1 onion, chopped
3 cloves garlic, minced
1 tablespoon vegetable oil
1 teaspoon oregano
2 cups chicken or vegetable broth
Salt to taste

Toast ancho peppers in a dry skillet over medium heat until slightly charred, about 1 minute per side. Remove from skillet and let cool. Add peppers to a blender or food processor and puree. Heat oil in a saucepan over medium heat. Add onion and garlic, and cook until onion is soft, about 5 minutes. Add oregano and cook for 1 minute. Gradually add broth while whisking constantly. Bring to a boil and reduce heat to low. Simmer for 10-15 minutes, stirring occasionally. Add pureed ancho peppers and season with salt to taste.

97. Guajillo Enchilada Sauce

2 dried guajillo chili peppers, stemmed and seeded
1 onion, chopped
3 cloves garlic, minced
1 tablespoon vegetable oil
1 teaspoon cumin
2 cups chicken or vegetable broth
Salt to taste

Toast guajillo peppers in a dry skillet over medium heat until slightly charred, about 1 minute per side. Remove from skillet and let cool. Add peppers to a blender or food processor and puree. Heat oil in a saucepan over medium heat. Add onion and garlic, and cook until onion is soft, about 5 minutes. Add cumin and cook for 1 minute. Gradually add broth while whisking constantly. Bring to a boil and reduce heat to low. Simmer for 10-15 minutes, stirring occasionally. Add pureed guajillo peppers and season with salt to taste.

98. Mole Enchilada Sauce

2 dried ancho chili peppers, stemmed and seeded
2 dried pasilla chili peppers, stemmed and seeded
1 onion, chopped
3 cloves garlic, minced
1 tablespoon vegetable oil
1/4 cup raisins
1/4 cup almonds, chopped
1/4 cup sesame seeds
1/4 teaspoon cinnamon
1/4 teaspoon cloves
1/4 teaspoon allspice
2 cups chicken or vegetable broth
Salt to taste

Toast ancho and pasilla peppers in a dry skillet over medium heat until slightly charred, about 1 minute per side. Remove from skillet and let cool. Add peppers to a blender or food processor and puree. Heat oil in a saucepan over medium heat. Add onion and garlic, and cook until onion is soft, about 5 minutes. Add raisins, almonds, sesame seeds, cinnamon, cloves, and allspice. Cook for 1 minute. Gradually add broth while whisking constantly. Bring to a boil and reduce heat to low. Simmer for 10-15 minutes, stirring occasionally. Add pureed pepper mixture and season with salt to taste.

99. Salsa Verde Enchilada Sauce

2 pounds tomatillos, husks removed
1 onion, chopped
3 cloves garlic, minced
1 jalapeño pepper, seeded and chopped
1/4 cup chopped cilantro
2 cups chicken or vegetable broth
Salt to taste

Place tomatillos in a large pot and cover with water. Bring to a boil over high heat. Reduce heat to low and simmer for 10-15 minutes, until tomatillos are tender. Drain and let cool. Add tomatillos to a blender or food processor and puree. Heat oil in a saucepan over medium heat. Add onion, garlic, and jalapeño, and cook until onion is soft, about 5 minutes. Add cilantro and cook for 1 minute. Gradually add broth while whisking constantly. Bring to a boil and reduce heat to low. Simmer for 10-15 minutes, stirring occasionally. Add pureed tomatillos and season with salt to taste.

100. Green Chile Enchilada Sauce

2 cans (4 ounces each) diced green chilies
1 onion, chopped
3 cloves garlic, minced
1 teaspoon cumin
2 cups chicken or vegetable broth
Salt to taste

Heat oil in a saucepan over medium heat. Add onion and garlic, and cook until onion is soft, about 5 minutes. Add cumin and cook for 1 minute. Gradually add broth while whisking constantly. Bring to a boil and reduce heat to low. Simmer for 10-15 minutes, stirring occasionally. Add diced green chilies and season with salt to taste.

CONCLUSION

Enchiladas are a classic and flavorful dish that is enjoyed by many people around the world. With their endless possibilities for fillings, sauces, and toppings, they can be customized to suit any taste preferences. Whether you prefer a meat-based filling or a vegetarian option, there is an enchilada recipe for everyone to enjoy. So next time you are in the mood for a hearty and satisfying meal, consider making some delicious enchiladas and let your taste buds be delighted.

www.ingramcontent.com/pod-product-compliance
Lightning Source LLC
LaVergne TN
LVHW021709060526
838200LV00050B/2576